At Home
Ross Burden

To my Grandmother for the ability
To my Mother for the motive
To Mel for the opportunity

At Home with Ross Burden

Delicious seasonal recipes
for entertaining friends

Ross Burden

metro

First published in Great Britain in 1998
by Metro Books (an imprint of Metro Publishing Limited), 19 Gerrard Street, London W1V 7LA

All rights reserved: no part of this publication may be reproduced, stored in a retrieval system, or transmitted in any form or by any means, electronic, mechanical, photocopying or otherwise, without the prior written consent of the publisher.

Text © 1998 Ross Burden

Ross Burden is hereby identified as the author of this work in accordance with Section 77 of the Copyright, Designs and Patents Act 1988.

British Library Cataloguing in Publication Data. A CIP record of this book is available on request from the British Library.

Editor: Norma MacMillan
Design: Roger Walker
Photography: Sian Irvine
Stylist: Joy Skipper

ISBN 1 900512 55 6

10 9 8 7 6 5 4 3 2 1

Typeset by SX Composing DTP, Rayleigh, Essex
Printed in Great Britain by Butler & Tanner Ltd, Frome

Contents

Acknowledgements vi

Introduction 1

Canapés 5

Starters 23

Fish 61

Poultry & Feathered Game 97

Meat 137

Vegetables 171

Puddings 197

Basic Recipes 227

Menus 235

Index 241

Acknowledgements

I could have made every dish in this book in a fraction of the time it took to write. I have developed a great awe of food writers who not only convey information and motivation but make it seem so effortless.

I would like to thank all my friends, especially my long-suffering flatmate Paul, for me being grumpier and grumpier as the deadline approached; my secretary, Kirsten, who took on the lion's share of the typing; and my agents, Carolynne and Michael.

Of course, the motivation for this book was all the people with whom I've eaten.

Buon appetito

Introduction

A companion is one with whom one breaks bread, and it is a great love of sharing good food with good company that inspired this book. I have no desire to write intricate and exquisitely difficult recipes in the manner of gastro-porn. To my mind there are two types of food, restaurant food and home food. This book is firmly rooted in the latter. The following dishes are some of my favourite things and are often seen on my table when I am joined there by friends.

Since my student days in Auckland, when my flatmates and I joined study benches in the garden and had open lunches (admission: 1 bottle potable red) for up to 30, I've been gripped by cooking for people. A great man, Brillat-Savarin, once said: 'Food made without love feeds only half the man.' I think that is the most splendid sentiment. How much nicer it is to have a slice of home-made cake with a cup of tea in the company of someone you care for than tea in a stuffy hotel. By cooking for people (which need not be difficult or costly) we show our willingness to spend time and effort for someone. How much more rare a treat that is.

The recipes are arranged by season in each section, to make the most of local produce and to keep variety alive. Since the advent of the year-round strawberry, I'm not sure that I've had more than a couple. Seasonal eating complements the weather too – salad in winter is out of place, as is a stew in summer, no matter how fashionable. Do feel free to substitute whatever you have or can find in the recipes; apart from the delicate chemistry of cake-making, there's little that cannot be fiddled with. If you prefer one herb to another, use it. If you can't find hake, use haddock. As long as the general texture, intensity of flavour and physical properties of the substitute are similar, give it a go.

I'm hugely thrifty and love a bargain. I often return from the supermarket with a 'find' and devise recipes for my swag. I wouldn't advocate sad, tired and past-it produce, but the sell-by dates on most hardy produce, such as vegetables, are vastly under-estimated. I found a red cabbage in the fridge, kept there for 5 months, that was perfectly good. We must remember that our grandmothers stored apples and vegetables through the winter without benefit of refrigeration. I once went to a market outside Prague where all the produce looked positively medieval – slightly lower in vitamins possibly, but full of flavour, unlike the varieties now bred for physical perfection rather than taste. How sad to trumpet about tomatoes 'grown for flavour'. What on earth else are they for ? As you step into an Italian greengrocer there is an odd musky smell, which transports me instantly back to my childhood in Hawkes Bay in New Zealand. It is the smell of tomato leaves. My father grew luscious tomatoes, ripened in the sun during hot summers, which were bottled and frozen for the rest of the year. All our food was local and seasonal by necessity. My grandmother had raspberry canes that bore their harvest for just 2 weeks a year. Such a treat – the fifty weeks of enforced abstinence made their arrival so much more exciting.

   I was brought up with bottling, pickling and preserving. The occasional treat of fish and chips was the only convenience food we had. I'm desperately against additives and preservatives, and really believe that simple, fresh food cooked from raw is the best diet. I love to eat meat, game and fish as long as the beast has had a nice life, and follow the Italian example of 'a little of the best'. Now that we have seen the costs of intensive farming, the movement towards lower yield and higher quality livestock is gaining momentum, and this is to be supported. Properly reared and hung meat, with dark cream fat and brown/red flesh, is so much more delicious than the 'supermarket red' version. Many people would see eating a pheasant, shot from the sky, as cruel, but how much nicer a free-range life it's had as against that of a battery chicken.

   My home town is on the coast (about 90 per cent of New Zealanders live less than 1 mile from the sea) and I was imbued with a love of fish and seafood. We used to gather sea-urchins, abalone and clams for supper and often ate rock lobster because it was cheap. The one gastronomic area Britain lags behind in is its general and blanket decision that it doesn't like fish (unless it's coated in batter and deep-fried). I've often been in Scotland and Norfolk and encountered people who wouldn't try fish – a strange attitude in two of the best fish-producing regions in Europe! In general people think of fish as 'fishy', but fresh fish shouldn't smell at all of anything more than the sea. Granted, fish isn't always cheap, but then we tend to stick to three or four types and ignore cheap and delicious species such as mackerel and whiting. Good farmed salmon (and sadly much isn't) represents great value for money and is full of the omega-3 oils essential to good health, especially for our hearts. I used to buy fresh white tuna when working in my last job as head chef at the Canal Brasserie. The fish would arrive fresh from Cornish waters less than 8 hours after being caught, and would be transformed into steaks to grill and trimmings for salade niçoise; the cook's treat was to shave off a little and have *sashimi* for breakfast.

The British and Irish cheese industries are a success beyond imagining. The brewing sector had CAMRA to shine a light, but cheeses have been invented, reinvented and developed by a set of individuals passionate about their craft. I am besotted by these wonderful products and their romantic names, such as Cooleeney, Gubeen, Tymsborough, Ticklemore and Innes. I was almost disappointed to learn that Yarg wasn't hundreds of years old, but was recently developed by the Gray family (Yarg backwards!). As our man Brillat-Savarin commented, 'dinner without cheese is like a woman with one eye'!

Travelling is my other passion, and you will find influences in these recipes from North Africa, Asia and Central America. With the boom in supermarkets' stock, there should be little trouble in finding the ingredients to make these dishes. If you need to go a bit further afield you'll find that Asian supermarkets are not only fun to visit but represent great value – spices bought in bulk are often a tenth of the cost of that in supermarkets. I make a point of buying anything I've not seen before and trying it out. Many of these recipes are the result of fiddling about with little more than what £5 will buy and 20 minutes of time!

I have spent many hours lost in conversation at table with loads of brilliant people and have made a career from it. I really hope you'll share these recipes with your family and friends soon.

Bien mange, bien bu, merci Jesu.

Note
Some recipes in this book use raw or undercooked eggs. Because of the risk of Salmonella poisoning, these recipes should be avoided by the elderly, young children, pregnant women and people whose immunity has been compromised by illness.

CANAPÉS

Spring

Thai Seafood Salad in Chicory

The bitterness of chicory makes it ideal for this canapé as it works so well with the clean taste of the seafood. The mix of seafood is entirely up to you and your supplier – mixtures of cooked seafood such as prawns, scallops, squid, mussels and cubes of white fish can be bought at deli counters. Just don't make the bites too big. It is possible to get red chicory in the spring and summer. If you see any, use it because it makes a brilliant counterpoint against the white seafood filling.

Makes 30
Preparation time: 10 minutes plus 30 minutes marinating

500g (1lb 2oz) mixed cooked seafood salad
2 tablespoons toasted sesame oil
2 tablespoons sweet chilli sauce
2 tablespoons fish sauce
2 tablespoons lime juice
2 tablespoons palm sugar *or* soft brown sugar
2 tablespoons chopped fresh coriander
2 tablespoons sesame seeds
12 fresh lime leaves, very finely shredded
3 heads chicory, leaves separated to make 30 neat 'boats'

- Mix together all the ingredients except the chicory. Leave to marinate for 30 minutes.
- Drain the seafood and fill the chicory 'boats'. Serve immediately.

Spring

Beancurd Crab Rolls with Sweet Chilli Dip

Beancurd sheets, a Chinese ingredient imported into Thai cuisine, are rather strange to use but give a delicious result. The sheets are really the skin that forms at the top of the vats when making tofu. This skin is scraped off and dried, so before use the sheets need to be soaked in warm water to soften. Their texture somewhat resembles rubber gloves! Being very pliable, ripped sheets can easily be mended with pieces from the rest of the pack. Chinese and Thai supermarkets stock beancurd sheets very inexpensively; there isn't a suitable replacement.

Makes about 60 pieces
Preparation time: 20 minutes plus cooling
Cooking time: 10 minutes

4 beancurd sheets, each about 15 x 30cm (6 × 12in)
170g (6oz) crabmeat
55g (2oz) minced pork
2 garlic cloves, finely chopped
2 tablespoons chopped fresh coriander
1 egg
1 tablespoon light soy sauce
½ teaspoon white pepper
1 teaspoon sugar
pinch of salt
oil for deep-frying
Sweet Chilli Dipping Sauce (see Duck and Ginger Wontons, page 14)

- Soak the beancurd sheets in cold water for about 10 minutes or until soft and pliable; drain.
- Meanwhile, thoroughly combine the crabmeat, pork, garlic, coriander, egg, soy sauce, pepper, sugar and salt. Divide the mixture into 4 portions.
- Lay a beancurd sheet on the work surface (handle carefully as the sheets tend to split, but don't worry if they do as you can patch the holes). Put one portion of crab mixture on to the top half of the sheet and shape the mixture into a sausage lying crossways. Wrap the beancurd sheet round the filling and roll up,

folding in the ends. Repeat, to make 4 rectangular parcels, each about 15cm (6in) long.
- Steam the parcels for about 10 minutes. Remove from the steamer and allow to cool. At this point you can set the parcels aside for final cooking later that day, or even the following day (they can also be frozen at this stage).
- To finish, cut each parcel into 10–15 pieces. Deep-fry in oil heated to 190°C/375°F or until a day-old cube of bread browns in 1 minute, until golden brown all over. Drain on kitchen paper and serve hot, with the dipping sauce.

Chef's tip

Disposable rubber gloves are very useful for tasks such as peeling artichokes or filleting fish.

SPRING

SEARED SCALLOPS WITH POORI AND BABA GANOUJ

This combines the sweet subtlety of fresh scallops with the smoky richness of the popular Middle-Eastern aubergine dip called baba ganouj. Poori are eaten in a myriad of forms as snacks all over India.

Makes 30
Preparation time: 20 minutes
Cooking time: 6 minutes

30 smallish scallops

For the poori
170g (6oz) plain flour
½ teaspoon ground cumin
½ teaspoon turmeric
½ teaspoon bicarbonate of soda
2 tablespoons sunflower oil, plus more for shallow frying

For the baba ganouj
1 aubergine
3 tablespoons tahini
2 garlic cloves, crushed
3 tablespoons extra virgin olive oil
juice of 2 lemons
black pepper

- To make the poori, sift the flour, spices and bicarbonate of soda into a bowl. Add 90ml (3floz) water and mix together. Add the oil, then mix in a little more more water, enough to form a light dough. Set aside to rest briefly
- Roll out the dough to a thickness of 5mm (¼in). Cut into 5cm (2in) rounds (you should have about 30). Shallow fry in hot sunflower oil for about 2 minutes or until golden on both sides and puffed. Drain on kitchen paper and reserve.
- Trim the scallops of any extraneous material, and remove the coral if preferred. (If it is retained, pierce it once so that it doesn't pop on contact with heat.)
- To make the baba ganouj, pierce the aubergine once, then grill for about 10 minutes, turning twice. (If you don't pierce it before cooking, it will explode

quite impressively and leave a horrendous mess to deal with. I can guarantee that this will happen only once!) When done, remove the stalk and peel under running water. Squeeze all the juices out of the flesh.
- Process the aubergine flesh with the tahini, garlic, oil, lemon juice and a little pepper in a blender or food processor to make a thick paste. Reserve.
- When ready to serve, sear the scallops on a hot griddle or in a frying pan, with only the slightest suggestion of oil, until browned, turning quickly to finish. (Scallops are horrid when overcooked, but will remain tender, sweet and juicy if treated with respect.)
- Spread or spoon a little of the aubergine paste over a poori, top with a scallop and serve immediately.

Canapés, clockwise from top left: Seared Scallops with Poori and Baba Ganouj (page 9); Chick Pea Fritters (page 22); Tartlets of Avocado Mousse and Quail's Eggs (page 15); Smoked Salmon Blinis (page 19); Moroccan Bread Pinwheels (page 11)

Watermelon, Chicory and Feta Salad (page 41)

Roasted Pepper and Aubergine Terrine (page 36)

Vichyssoise with Oyster and Caviar (page 24)

Summer

Moroccan Bread Pinwheels

This is a canapé I devised for the Turner Prize party. It has the festive colours of red, green and white, but with a really exotic and exciting twist. This is easily prepared in the morning and then sliced and served at the last moment. Markouk *is an unleavened North African bread, also called* lavash, *that can be bought from halal butchers as well as delis and food halls. It is great rolled with all sorts of fillings – try roast chicken, salad and saffron mayo.*

Makes 15
Preparation time: 5 minutes

1 sheet *markouk* or *lavash* (Moroccan bread)
150g (5½oz) soft fresh goat's cheese
1 jar sun-dried tomatoes, drained
15g (½oz) fresh mint leaves

- Choose an unripped sheet of *markouk* (it usually it comes in packets of three sheets and the middle one is often dodgy). Spread over the goat's cheese into a rectangular shape, avoiding the very edges of the bread which tend to be thicker.
- Purée the drained tomatoes in a blender or food processor. Spread the purée over the goat's cheese.
- Scatter with the mint, then roll up tightly from a long side, like a Swiss roll. At this point it can be chilled, or serve it straight away cut into oblique slices.

Summer

Baby Potatoes and Caviar

These really are the most fantastic canapés, and I've served them at the smartest of parties. At the beginning of the British potato season, potatoes have the best flavour. I know this is an expensive thing to serve, but please don't be tempted to substitute lumpfish roe for the caviar – it might help to know that lumpfish roe is white until dyed red or black. Flyingfish or salmon roes are delicious and cheaper if you want an alternative to the caviar.

Makes 30
Preparation time: 10 minutes
Cooking time: 25 minutes

30 perfect baby potatoes, cleaner than clean	80g (scant 3oz) crème fraîche
	50g (scant 2oz) beluga *or* sevruga caviar

- Preheat the oven to 180°C/350°F/Gas 4.
- Bake the potatoes just as you would larger ones, allowing about 25 minutes. Leave to cool slightly. (If the potatoes are too hot they'll melt the crème fraîche and you'll lose the whole point.)
- When cool enough to handle, cut a cross in the top of each potato and squeeze open to form a volcano shape. Spoon a little crème fraîche into each and top with a little caviar. (It is important not to use metal with caviar as it picks up the metallic taste, so use a plastic or other spoon – I have even eaten beluga from an obscenely large tin with my fingers.)

SUMMER

Prawn Tempura with Wasabi

Tempura has very much come of age and is now part of the drinks circuit menu. Tempura doesn't like to sit though, so is best made in smaller batches, otherwise the steam generated by the hot prawns or vegetables softens the crisp batter. (Packets of tempura mix are easily obtainable.) Wasabi is Japanese green horseradish and has quite a kick. It is now widely sold in powdered form or ready mixed into a paste for sushi. Either one is fine for this recipe, but note that the powder is stronger than the paste.

Makes 30
Preparation time: 8 minutes
Cooking time: 10 minutes

30 raw medium-sized prawns
100g (3½oz) tempura batter mix
sunflower oil for deep-frying
salt and pepper

For the dipping sauce
125g (4½oz) crème fraîche
1 tablespoon *wasabi* powder, or to taste

- Peel the prawns, leaving the last tail section on. Devein.
- Make the batter according to the instructions on the packet, to achieve a consistency like double cream.
- Dip the prawns into the batter, then let any excess drip off. Deep-fry in oil heated to 190°C/375°F or until a day-old cube of bread browns in 1 minute, until puffed and golden brown all over. Drain well on kitchen paper. Season with salt and pepper.
- Serve immediately, with the crème fraîche well mixed with the *wasabi*.

Summer

Duck and Ginger Wontons

Wontons, a fixture of Chinese restaurants for many years, have now found their way into most supermarkets as ready-prepared nibbles. However, you can make your own very easily and they will cost a fraction of the bought ones. Essentially a deep-fried ravioli, the pasta-like wrapper ekes out a filling which must be quite highly flavoured. In this case duck is used, which can be trimmings or leftovers. A number of shapes are possible, but I think triangles are the most impressive. Wonton wrappers can be bought cheaply from Chinese and other oriental supermarkets (as can pickled ginger). They can be kept in the freezer for up to a month, but then become brittle.

Makes about 30
Preparation time: 20 minutes
Cooking time: 10 minutes

1 duck breast, skinned and all fat and sinew removed
2 tablespoons pickled ginger
1 tablespoon soy sauce
2 tablespoons chopped fresh coriander
1 packet wonton wrappers
sunflower oil for deep-frying

For the sweet chilli dipping sauce
1 fresh chilli, finely chopped
2 garlic cloves, finely chopped
2 tablespoons sugar
2 tablespoons rice vinegar

- Combine the duck, ginger, soy sauce and coriander in a food processor and process to a well blended but still coarse texture.
- Place teaspoonfuls of the duck mixture on the centre of each wonton wrapper and fold into a triangle or money-bag shape.
- Deep-fry in oil heated to 190°C/375°F or until a day-old cube of bread browns in 1 minute, until golden all over. Drain on kitchen paper and serve immediately with the dipping sauce.
- To make the dipping sauce, boil all the ingredients together until thickened. Remove from the heat and cool.

Autumn

Tartlets of Avocado Mousse and Quail's Eggs

Quail's eggs were made for canapés as they're perfectly miniaturized versions of the egg. Most large supermarkets now stock them at very low prices. They pose a slight problem to peel in as much as the shell is thin and the membrane thick, in direct contrast to hen's eggs, but after a little practice you can easily tear through the peeling. When I do large cocktail parties, we all share the task and make a game of it. For this dish they need to be hard-boiled, but if served on their own – say with celery salt – they're much nicer if soft-boiled for just 2 minutes 15 seconds. I suggest you buy the tiny tartlets cases now sold by delis and supermarkets rather than making your own.

Makes 24
Preparation time: 12 minutes

12 quail's eggs
24 bought tartlet cases
24 small sprigs of fresh chervil

For the avocado mousse
1 ripe avocado

a 425g (15oz) can chick peas, drained
1 tablespoon extra virgin olive oil
juice of 1 lemon
2 garlic cloves, crushed
2 tablespoons tahini
salt and pepper

- Hard-boil the quail's eggs for 3 minutes, then drain and refresh in iced water.
- Purée the avocado flesh and chick peas with the oil, lemon juice, garlic and tahini in a blender or food processor. Season with salt and pepper.
- Peel the eggs and cut in half lengthways.
- Put a small spoonful of the avocado mousse in each tartlet case and top with an egg half. Garnish with the chervil and serve.

Autumn

Celeriac Crisps with Finnan Sashimi

The very ugly but very tasty celeriac has made rather a fashionable leap forward over the last few years. More power to it, as it really is a splendid vegetable. I'm not entirely sure how I discovered finnan haddock was good raw – I can only think that it smelled so damn good one morning when it arrived that I was tempted to forgo the usual cooking processes!

Makes 36
Preparation time: 14 minutes
Cooking time: 16 minutes

1 large celeriac, heavy for its size
1 large finnan haddock, skinned
80g (scant 3oz) mascarpone
75ml (2½floz) horseradish sauce
sunflower oil for deep-frying
15 fresh chives, halved on the slant
white pepper

- Peel the celeriac and cut into 6 wedges, trimming away any spongy material from the centre. (As you work, keep the pieces of celeriac in a bowl of water acidulated with lemon juice to prevent discoloration.) Take six 8mm (⅓in) thick slices from the central portion of each segment; keep the rest for mash.
- Trim the haddock, removing bones or sinew, and slice 36 thin flakes of flesh.
- Whisk the mascarpone until fluffy, then fold the horseradish through.
- Deep-fry the celeriac slices in sunflower oil heated to 180°C/350°F, to blanch, remove and drain. Raise the temperature of the oil to 190°C/375°F (see page 14) and deep-fry the celeriac again to crisp up and brown. Drain on kitchen paper and cool.
- To finish, top each celeriac crisp with a little of the horseradish cream and a piece of chive. Lay a haddock flake on the top and season with white pepper. Serve immediately.

Autumn

Moroccan Fishcakes and Harissa

I often make Thai fishcakes for cocktail parties and as a starter, but I am so bored with them that I decided to change the flavourings from curry paste and coriander to more north African ones, such as preserved lemons, harissa and mint. The lemons are dropped and the following mixture is the one I like the best. Harissa is now available in supermarkets across the country.

Makes about 60
Preparation time: 30 minutes
Cooking time: 30 minutes

1 kg (2¼lb) unblanched almonds
2kg (4½lb) white fish fillets
50g (1¾oz) fresh mint leaves
1 tablespoon harissa paste
250ml (8½floz) olive oil

250ml (8½floz) sunflower oil
sunflower oil for deep-frying

To serve
harissa sauce
Fresh Tomato Sauce (see page 228)

- Grind the almonds in a food processor until they resemble a breadcrumb texture. Tip into a large bowl.
- Process the fish until it forms into a ball in the processor. Add to the bowl.
- Put all the other ingredients into the processor and mix together, then tip into the bowl. Mix everything together thoroughly.
- Form the mixture into egg-shaped cakes. Deep-fry in oil heated to 190°C/375°F or until a day-old cube of bread browns in 1 minute, until a deep brown all over. Drain on kitchen paper.
- Serve hot, with harissa for the brave and a fresh tomato sauce for the less so.

Winter

Pork-stuffed Mild Chillies

By using mild chillies, you can eat all but the stalks in one go. The caribe chillies now available are perfect for these canapés.

Makes 12 pieces
Preparation time: 12 minutes
Cooking time: 12 minutes

6 mild yellow chillies
170g (6oz) minced pork
6 fresh lime leaves, finely shredded
3 garlic cloves, finely chopped
1 tablespoon finely chopped fresh coriander
1 stem lemongrass, tender part sliced
2 teaspoons light soy sauce
¼ teaspoon white pepper
1 teaspoon toasted sesame oil
½ teaspoon salt

- Preheat the oven to 180°C/350°F/Gas 4.
- Slice the chillies lengthways in half, leaving the stalks on, and remove the core and all the seeds.
- Mix together all the other ingredients and stuff into the chilli boats. Arrange on a baking tray.
- Bake on the top shelf of the oven for 12 minutes. Serve hot.

Winter

Pitta Crisps with Houmous and Tahini Yogurt

I had this brilliant idea for nibbles whilst staying with friends in their barn in Yorkshire. I was ravenous while making dinner, and the only snacky bits seemed to be some stale pitta bread, a scrap of Parmesan and some Greek yogurt. There's more than a hint of student about these, but they're delicious all the same.

Makes about 50
Preparation time: 15 minutes
Cooking time: 15 minutes

6 pitta breads
75g (2½oz) butter
75g (2½oz) Parmesan, freshly grated
1 teaspoon cayenne pepper
juice of 2 lemons
4 tablespoons tahini
500g (1lb 2oz) Greek yogurt

a few drops of Tabasco sauce
paprika
a 425g (15oz) can chick peas, drained
3 garlic cloves, crushed
100ml (3½floz) olive oil
1 teaspoon cumin seeds
salt and pepper

- Preheat the oven to 200°C/400°F/Gas 6.
- Split the breads open. Mix the butter with the cheese and cayenne, and spread over the 12 pitta halves on the rough side. Cut each half more or less neatly into 6 or so pieces. Bake for 15 minutes or until crisp.
- Meanwhile, whisk half the lemon juice into half the tahini with 1 teaspoon salt. Stir into the yogurt with the Tabasco. Pile into a bowl and dust with paprika.
- Put the remaining tahini and lemon juice in a blender or food processor with the chick peas, garlic and oil. Process until smooth, thinning with a little water if necessary. Season with the cumin seeds, salt and pepper. Pile into another bowl and drizzle with a little more oil.
- Serve the crisps around the outside of the two dips.

Winter

Smoked Salmon Blinis

The classic canapé, this smoked salmon nibble remains as stylish as ever, and when the 'knot' is perfected it will impress your friends enormously. Traditionally, yeast-leavened blinis are used, but this recipe uses much easier Scotch pancake batter flavoured with dill. The price of smoked salmon is falling, but watch the quality closely. It shouldn't be greasy or smelly and should have very little visible fat – thick bands of fat on cheap salmon signifies a fish that has been farmed to swim lazily in a tank, developing no flavour. Fish farmed in swiftly running water will have taut muscle, little fat and a more 'wild' flavour.

Makes 30
Preparation time: 20 minutes
Cooking time: 15 minutes

For the dill blinis
2 eggs
2 tablespoons caster sugar
pinch of salt
225g (8oz) plain flour
1 tablespoon chopped fresh dill
2 teaspoons baking powder
about 250ml (8½floz) milk

butter for cooking

For the topping
400g (14oz) smoked salmon strips
150g (5½oz) crème fraîche
100g (3½oz) keta *or* salmon roe (optional)
30 tiny sprigs of fresh dill

- To make the blinis, whisk the eggs with the sugar and salt. Sift in half of the flour and mix well, then add the rest of the flour, the dill and baking powder. Loosen with the milk. The consistency of the batter should be that of soured cream.
- Melt a tiny amount of butter in a heavy frying pan and swirl to coat. Cook tablespoons of the batter until bubbles appear, then flip over and cook the second side for 30 seconds. As the blinis are cooked, remove them from the pan. Allow to cool.
- To knot the salmon, cut 30 pieces, each 2 × 15cm (¾ × 6in), and wind around the second and middle fingers of one hand. Hold together, then neatly turn

almost inside-out so that a hat or cushion of salmon is formed. (These can be stored, covered, for several hours.)
- Top each blini with a teaspoon of crème fraîche and then a salmon knot. A final luxurious touch is a few salmon eggs and then a sprig of dill to garnish.

> ## Chef's tip
> *Keep all the trimmings from the smoked salmon and blend with an equal quantity of mascarpone. Season with lemon juice and black pepper. Serve as smoked salmon pâté with toast or crackers.*

Winter

Chick pea Fritters with Carrot Shreds

These are effectively falafel dressed up for a smart party, and are always really well received at drinks receptions. The fritters can be served on their own with the yogurt or with a salad as a starter.

Makes 12
Preparation time: 30 minutes
Cooking time: 8 minutes

2 carrots, peeled and cut into thin spaghetti-like shreds
2 tablespoons honey
4 tablespoons cider vinegar
salt and pepper

For the fritters
a 425g (15oz) can chick peas
2 tablespoons tahini
juice of 1 lemon
1 teaspoon cumin seeds
1 tablespoon fresh mint leaves
1 tablespoon parsley leaves
sunflower oil for deep-frying

For the topping
200g (7oz) Greek yogurt
1 tablespoon tahini
1 tablespoon lemon juice
12 fresh chives, halved

- Dress the carrot shreds with the honey and vinegar, season and leave to soften for 30 minutes.
- To make the fritters, put the chick peas, tahini, lemon juice, cumin seeds and herbs in a blender or food processor and process into a soft paste. With floured hands, form into 3–4cm (1¼–1½in) patties. Deep-fry in oil heated to 190°C/375°F or until a day-old cube of bread browns in 1 minute, until golden all over. Drain on kitchen paper and keep warm.
- Whisk the yogurt with the tahini and lemon juice and season well.
- Top each warm fritter with a little tahini yogurt, then carrot and two halves of chive. Season again and serve.

STARTERS

Spring

Vichyssoise with Oyster and Caviar

This is one of my favourite soups. The caviar can be left out, as can the oysters, but they add a delicious counterpoint. The soup can be prepared up to the addition of the cream and then frozen, or chilled for a day.

Serves 6
Preparation time: 35 minutes plus chilling
Cooking time: 20 minutes
3 small leeks
2 medium potatoes

30g (1oz) butter
2 tablespoons chopped parsley
1.5 litres (2¾ pints) chicken stock
300ml (10floz) double cream
salt and pepper

6 heaped teaspoons crème fraîche
6 large fresh oysters, shucked
25g (scant 1oz) caviar

- Remove all tough and dirty parts of the leeks, then slice thinly. Peel the potatoes and finely slice to 2mm (¹⁄₁₆–⅛in) or so in thickness.
- Cook the leeks gently in the butter until softened but not coloured. Add the potatoes, parsley, stock and several grinds of black pepper. Simmer for 20 minutes or until the leeks and potatoes are soft.
- Allow to cool and then purée in a blender or food processor in batches. Pass through a fine sieve into a bowl. Add the cream and 1 teaspoon salt and stir. (The amount of salt may sound excessive, but this soup is best eaten very cold, which robs some of the flavour; this is made up for by the salt.) Chill very well.
- To serve, place a heaped teaspoon of crème fraîche in the centre of six chilled soup plates and pour the soup around it. Top with an oyster and then with a little caviar.

SPRING

Roquefort Parfait with Chestnut Honey

This is a very easy starter that can be prepared well in advance. Roquefort, a piquant blue ewes' milk cheese, is traditionally served with honey. It may sound a strange combination, but believe me, it works. I discovered chestnut honey in Tuscany and have become hooked. It has a rather savoury, smoky flavour which is better here than a lighter, floral variety. Do try it. This would be great with wholemeal bread or melba toast.

Serves 8
Preparation time: 10 minutes plus at least 8 hours chilling

250g (9oz) cream cheese
1 tablespoon extra virgin olive oil
10g (scant ¼oz) fresh basil, shredded
200g (7oz) Roquefort cheese

chopped fresh herbs (optional)
8 tablespoons chestnut honey
white pepper

- Beat the cream cheese in an electric mixer until light and fluffy, about 4 minutes. Add the oil, basil and half the Roquefort and season well with white pepper. Beat to a smooth consistency.
- Chop the remaining Roquefort into 1cm (½in) cubes and fold through the mixture to maintain the chunkiness.
- Take a piece of foil 1 metre (3ft) long and fold it in half lengthways. Oil the foil well. The foil can be sprinkled with chopped fresh herbs for a smarter finish to the parfait.
- Spoon the cheese mixture along the length of the foil, to form a cylinder 4–5cm (1¾–2in) across. Fold up the cheese mixture in the foil, then roll the package gently on a flat surface to make a neat log shape. Twist the ends. Chill well for at least 8 hours to firm up.
- When ready to serve, unwrap and cut into 16 neat slices. Drizzle with the chestnut honey.

SPRING

TARTE TATIN NIÇOISE

These were invented as a tasty starter for a kosher dinner and have become a firm favourite. If serving kosher-observing or vegetarian friends, check the pastry before you buy it, because most brands are made with lard! I would recommend using anchovies in brine, which you can find sold from plastic containers in deli chill cabinets. They are less salty than canned anchovies.

Serves 6
Preparation time: 30 minutes
Cooking time: 12–15 minutes

50g (scant 2oz) butter
18 cherry tomatoes, halved
1 yellow pepper, roasted and peeled (see Roasted Pepper and Aubergine Terrine, page 36) then cut into 18 long slices
6 canned artichoke hearts, cut into quarters
18 Kalamata olives (or similar), stoned
12 anchovy fillets
36 baby capers, rinsed and dried
1 tablespoon fresh thyme leaves
250g (9oz) puff pastry
black pepper

To garnish
1 tablespoon balsamic vinegar
4 tablespoons olive oil
100g (3½oz) rocket leaves

- Use the butter to grease 6 non-stick tartlet tins of 10cm (4in) diameter. Chill to harden the butter.
- Arrange the vegetables, olives, anchovies and capers on the bottoms of the tins, remembering that they will not move during cooking and will appear in exactly the same way when turned out for serving. It will help to place the largest items, such as the slices of pepper, first and finish with the smallest, in other words the capers. The slices of pepper and anchovy fillets are very effective if wound round the tomatoes or olives. Season well with black pepper and the fresh thyme leaves.
- Roll out the pastry to a thickness of 3mm (⅛in) and cut out 6 circles of 12cm (5in) diameter. Lay a circle on each of the tins and push down around the contents. Once done, repeat and tighten the edges so that each tart has a flat top

and complete rim of 1cm (½in) all the way round the filling (as the tarts will be inverted after cooking, the finish is important).
- Refrigerate the completed tarts until ready to cook (they can be kept in the fridge for up to a day).
- Preheat the oven to 200°C/400°F/Gas 6.
- Bake, straight from the fridge, for 12–15 minutes or until the pastry is browned and the filling has started to be fragrant. Invert on to the serving plates so the pastry is on the bottom.
- Quickly mix the vinegar into the oil and dress the rocket. Garnish each plate with a small bunch of rocket and serve immediately.

Wine note

A light, earthy red, such as a good Chianti or a Bardolino, would be delicious with these tarts.

Spring

Potted Shrimps

The first time I potted shrimps was at the behest of a well-known peer who loves antique motorcars. I had no idea how many of these succulent little shrimps it would take to make potted shrimps for 30, nor how long they would take to shell! Brown Morecombe shrimps are bought cooked, so all you have to do is peel them and set them in butter. I suggest you do this in front of the TV with a drink (or two) at hand. It's worth the effort because the flavour is unparalleled.

Serves 6
Preparation time: 1 hour

450g (1lb) unsalted butter
450g (1lb) freshly cooked brown shrimps, peeled
pinch of ground mace
pinch of chilli powder
pinch of freshly ground white pepper

- Melt the butter over a low heat until it foams. Remove from the heat and skim off and discard the froth from the top of the butter. Pour the now clear liquid, or 'clarified', butter into a bowl, discarding the dregs at the bottom of the pan (these dregs are the milk proteins, which have a very low burning point).
- Reserve about one-third of the clarified butter and mix the rest with the shrimps and spices. Spoon into 6 ramekin dishes and allow to cool.
- When the dishes are thoroughly cold, heat the reserved clarified butter to liquefy it, then pour over the shrimps to seal. (To be rather grand, fresh tarragon leaves can be set in the top layer of butter.) Keep in the fridge, and serve at cool room temperature, with melba toast.

Wine note

Try this with a cold glass of Manzanilla, the salty, nutty version of fino sherry.

Spring

Guinea Fowl, Leek and Potato Terrine

Terrines of all kinds are a favourite of mine, and I think that the finest to be found in London are at L'Oranger. Ready Steady Cook *had a Christmas party there for which the chef, Marcus Wareing, produced a terrine of foie gras, truffles, potatoes and ox tongue – two luxury ingredients and two more commonplace. It was one of the best things I've ever eaten. The ingredients in this terrine are far more prosaic (except for the optional truffle), but almost as delicious.*

Serves 10
Preparation time: 40 minutes plus 24 hours weighting and setting
Cooking time: 2 hours

800g (1¾lb) leeks
800g (1¾lb) large baking potatoes, peeled
6 guinea fowl breasts, skinned
100g (3½oz) butter, cut into 12 slices
20g (¾oz) fresh white *or* black truffle, thinly sliced (optional)
salt and pepper
walnut oil to finish

- Preheat the oven to 150°C/300°F/Gas 2. Oil a 24 × 10 × 7.5cm (9½ × 4 x 3in) loaf tin.
- Trim the leeks and halve lengthways. Blanch in boiling salted water for 2 minutes, then refresh and drain on a tea cloth.
- Trim the potatoes into neat rectangular shapes, then cut into 5mm (¼in) thick slices. Blanch in boiling salted water for 5 minutes; refresh and drain.
- Pound the guinea fowl breasts under cling film until half the original thickness.
- Line the bottom and sides of the loaf tin with a single layer of leeks, slightly overlapping them. There should be enough extending up over the rim to fold over the top when done. The easiest way to do this is to lay the leeks from one side and then the other, repeating alternately.

Starters

- Lay a single layer of overlapping potato slices on top of the leeks. Fit 2 of the guinea fowl breasts over the potatoes. Season well and lay 4 slices of butter on the breasts. Top with some truffle slices, if using. Any left-over leeks can be put in lengthways now before adding another layer of potatoes and then more guinea fowl, butter and truffles. Repeat the layers once more. End with potatoes and close with the leeks.
- Cover with oiled foil and place in a roasting tray filled with enough water to come half way up the sides of the loaf tin. Cook in the oven for 2 hours, then test with a metal skewer. The terrine should not have too much resistance as the skewer goes in. After 30 seconds remove the skewer, which should feel quite hot. (If you have an instant-read thermometer, the internal temperature of the terrine should be 67°C/152°F.)
- Leave to cool to room temperature, then place the tin on a tray and weight down the terrine. Leave to set in the fridge for 24 hours.
- Serve sliced and drizzled with walnut oil, with salad and bread.

Wine note

A crisp Sauvignon Blanc or Chenin Blanc from South Africa would be a splendid pairing.

Spring

Sauté of Chorizo, Prawns and Beans

This southern Spanish idea is perfect for lazy outdoor cooking as there's very little to do. Supermarkets now sell huge, raw king prawn tails which are just delicious, but you could throw in some cooked ones for an even easier life. Chorizo comes in a slicing version and a smaller 'cooking' version. The latter, which is for stews and suchlike, is usually made of a much lower grade of pork, so I always use the slicing one.

Serves 6
Preparation time: 20 minutes
Cooking time: 12 minutes

400g (14oz) slicing chorizo, in a piece
3 tablespoons good olive oil
24 raw king prawns, the bigger the better, peeled
400g (14oz) shelled fresh broad beans, blanched and skinned, *or* frozen broad beans, thawed
juice of 2 lemons
3 tablespoons finely chopped fresh flat-leaf parsley
oil for brushing
12 thin slices French bread
pepper *or* dried chilli flakes

- Preheat the oven to 200°C/400°F/Gas 6.
- Cut the chorizo into sticks about 5cm (2in) long and 1cm ($\frac{1}{2}$in) thick. Heat the oil in a large frying pan and gently sauté the chorizo sticks until lightly browned all over. Remove and drain on kitchen paper. Pour away most of the oil left in the pan.
- Add the prawns to the pan and sauté for a couple of minutes on each side or until pink, but do not overcook or they'll be rubbery.
- Return the chorizo to the pan together with the broad beans, lemon juice and parsley. Season well with pepper or, possibly, a pinch of chilli flakes. Leave to heat through gently.

- Meanwhile, brush a non-stick baking tray with oil and then brush oil on the slices of bread. Toast in the oven for 10 minutes or so until lightly browned and crisped.
- Serve the sauté on a large platter, or in individual portions in soup plates, with the croutons.

Wine note

The 'greenness' of the dish suggests a vinho verde from Portugal, although a Sauvignon Blanc from New Zealand or Australia would also work very well.

Summer Panzanella

A peasant dish that has gained almost cult status in the Chiantishire set, Panzanella is best made from stale, coarse-textured bread. The best bread to use is ciabatta, which luckily goes stale almost immediately – bread in Italy tends to be sold stale so you're one step ahead. If you only have fresh bread, toast it under a grill lightly after dicing it. The choice of vegetables used in the salad doesn't really matter. It's the piquancy of the dressing that gives it such a zing!

Serves 8
Preparation time: 30 minutes plus 30 minutes chilling

1 loaf Italian bread *or* 2 loaves ciabatta, cut into 5mm (¼in) chunks
1 red onion, finely diced
12 ripe plum tomatoes, cut into 1cm (½in) pieces
3 yellow peppers, cut into 1cm (½in) pieces
½ cucumber, cut into 1cm (½in) chunks

For the dressing
3 large garlic cloves, crushed
6 anchovy fillets, finely diced
15g (½oz) fresh basil leaves
1 dried red chilli, seeded and crumbled
3 tablespoons sherry or red wine vinegar
170ml (scant 6floz) olive oil
salt and pepper

- Put the bread in a large bowl and sprinkle with enough water to moisten it, but not to make it mushy. Mix in all the vegetables.
- To make the dressing, grind the garlic, anchovies, basil and chilli to a paste in a mortar and pestle. Add the vinegar and then the oil and mix well. Season.
- Dress the salad, then chill for 30 minutes.
- Serve as a first course or as an accompaniment to cold cooked meats.

Summer

Spinach and Ricotta Malfatti

Gnocchi are my all-time favourite comfort food, either the potato- or the ricotta-based versions. Ginocchio means knee in Italian, and it is the dimples on either side of these dumplings that give them this name. There is the most wonderful restaurant in Sienna called La Logge which famously makes large versions of these, called malfatti *(badly made) due to their uneven shape. In their defence I can only say they're like Siennese biscuits –* brutti ma buoni *(ugly but good)!*

Serves 8
Preparation time: 25 minutes
Cooking time: 40 minutes

1 small onion, finely chopped
25g (scant 1oz) pancetta, chopped
25g (scant 1oz) butter
300g (10½oz) frozen spinach
pinch of salt
250g (9oz) ricotta
90g (3¼oz) plain flour
1 egg, beaten

80g (scant 3oz) Parmesan, freshly grated
¼ teaspoon grated nutmeg

To serve
Fresh Tomato Sauce (see page 228)
freshly grated Parmesan
chopped fresh herbs (optional)
black pepper (optional)

- Fry the onion with the pancetta in the butter until softened. Add the spinach and salt and cook for a further 5 minutes. Allow to cool.
- Beat the ricotta with the flour. Add the rest of the ingredients, including the spinach mixture, and mix very well.
- Flour a large surface. Form sausages of the ricotta and spinach mixture about 2cm (¾in) thick, turning them in the flour to prevent sticking. Cut into 2cm (¾in) lengths, pinch each one and dust with flour.

- Drop into a large pan of boiling salted water and poach until the dumplings float to the surface. Drain well. Serve hot with the tomato sauce and Parmesan.
- Alternatively, after poaching place in a buttered ovenproof dish, ladle over the tomato sauce, sprinkle with herbs, black pepper and Parmesan, and bake in an oven preheated to 200°C/400°F/Gas 6 for 20 minutes.

Chef's tip

When chopping onions, cut them in half, leaving the root end intact. This will keep the half together as you chop.

Summer

Roasted Pepper and Aubergine Terrine

I first made this in Tuscany, where I was staying with friends outside the glorious city of Sienna. The terrine was served as the first course at a lunch party for my friends' neighbours, who had come from their palazzo in Santa Columba, across the valley from us. The meal was simple yet memorable, with a mix of extraordinary people and a breath-taking view.

Serves 10
Preparation time: 1½ hours plus 12–24 hours weighting

10 ripe red peppers, the longer the better
2 ripe aubergines, each about 200g (7oz), cut lengthways into 5mm (¼in) slices
6 tablespoons olive oil
300ml (10floz) white wine vinegar
125g (4½oz) sugar
2 mace blades
12 black peppercorns
300g (10½oz) fresh white breadcrumbs
3 tablespoons toasted pine nuts
200g (7oz) feta cheese, cut into 2cm (¾in) cubes
15g (½oz) fresh mint leaves, finely shredded
salt and pepper

- Preheat the grill to high.
- Cut each of the peppers along its natural contours into 3–5 pieces, and remove the core, seeds and white membranes. Set the pieces on a baking tray, skin side up, and grill until the skin is blackened and bubbling all over. Remove the peppers to a polythene bag, or bowl covered with cling film, and allow to cool. Once cool, the skin can be removed very easily.
- While the peppers are cooling, salt the aubergine slices generously and leave for 30 minutes. (The salting process is not to remove bitterness, which should not be present in the fresh, ripe vegetable, but instead acts as a deterrent to

absorption later. By salting the aubergines, the cells pop and lose their ability to act as a sponge to oil, and thus will give a far lighter, less greasy result.)
- Rinse the aubergine slices, then drain and dry. Heat a little of the oil in a frying pan and fry the aubergine slices until lightly browned on both sides (do this in batches and add more oil to the pan as needed). Drain the slices on kitchen paper.
- Combine the vinegar, sugar, mace, peppercorns and 1 teaspoon salt in a saucepan and bring to the boil. Boil to dissolve the sugar and infuse the spices. Strain into a large bowl and leave to cool. When cooled, add the aubergine slices to the vinegar mixture and toss lightly. Allow to sit for a few minutes.
- Mix together the breadcrumbs, pine nuts, feta and mint. Season to taste with salt and pepper.
- Line a 20 × 10cm (8 × 4in) terrine mould or loaf tin with cling film. Arrange the peeled pepper pieces, skinned side up, over the bottom and up the sides of the mould to cover completely and extend above the top of the mould. Then line the bottom and sides with the aubergine slices. (If this seems difficult, you can make 2 layers of pepper alternating with 2 layers of aubergine; the aubergine will anchor the peppers in place.) Fill the centre with the feta mixture and moisten it with a little olive oil. Fold the aubergine slices and then the pepper pieces over the filling.
- Cover the top with cling film. Set a piece of card, cut to fit, over the top and weight it. Chill for 12–24 hours.
- Serve the terrine cut into slices, with toasted sourdough bread and salad.

Wine note

With all the flavours in this dish, any red or white would be suitable, but the cheaper the better.

Summer

Chicken Liver Parfait with Caramelized Orange

A great 1970s standby, chicken liver pâté (or parfait to the posh) is a favourite of mine. The melting sweetness combines so fantastically with melba toast. I often make it for Glyndebourne. Have picnic, will travel.

Serves 12–16
Preparation time: 30 minutes plus 1–2 hours cooling
Cooking time: 1 hour 20 minutes

400g (14oz) fresh chicken livers
8 shallots, chopped
1 garlic clove, chopped
1 sprig of fresh thyme
400g (14oz) plus 1 teaspoon unsalted butter
50ml (scant 2floz) cognac
100ml (3½floz) dry Madeira
100ml (3½floz) port
5 eggs
1 tablespoon salt
1 teaspoon freshly ground white pepper
melted dripping *or* cooking fat to seal

For the garnish
4 oranges
125g (4½oz) caster sugar
2 tablespoons green peppercorns packed in brine, drained

- Order fresh chicken livers well in advance and ask your butcher to remove the gall. (If the galls are still attached to the chicken livers, cut the flesh away from them. If any of the bitter liquid from the gall touches the liver, wash thoroughly.) If the livers are dark, soak them in milk for 1 day to remove all traces of blood. Wash, drain and pat dry before using.
- Preheat the oven to 150°C/300°F/Gas 2.
- In a medium saucepan, sweat the chopped shallots, garlic and thyme in the 1 teaspoon butter without colouring. Add the cognac, Madeira and port and bring to the boil. Reduce the liquid to about 4 tablespoons. Set aside.
- Melt the remaining butter slowly in a small saucepan.

- Purée the chicken livers in a food proccessor for 1 minute, then add the cooked shallot mixture and process to mix. Add the eggs, salt, pepper and, lastly, the melted butter. Blend for a few more seconds until the mixture is thoroughly amalgamated.
- Using the back of a ladle, force the mixture through a fine conical sieve into a terrine or loaf tin measuring 20 × 15cm (8 × 6in). Cover with buttered greaseproof paper.
- Line a deep roasting tin with foil. Set the terrine in the tin and pour in enough hot water to come three-quarters of the way up the sides of the terrine. Cook in the oven for 1 hour and 20 minutes. Check the oven temperature with a thermometer (do not trust the thermostat); if it rises above 150°C/300°F/Gas 2, the pâté will become overcooked and grey. To check if the pâté is cooked, insert a metal skewer into the centre, leave it for 2 seconds and then withdraw it; it should be hot and dry.
- Remove the cooked pâté from the oven and leave to cool at room temperature for 1–2 hours.
- Seal with a little melted fat to prevent discoloration, then allow to rest in the fridge for 1 day before serving.
- For the garnish, peel and segment the oranges, retaining any juice. Make a caramel with the sugar and 100ml (3½floz) water; when well coloured, add the reserved orange juice and stir over a low heat to dissolve. Leave to cool, then marinate the orange segments for 10 minutes. Just before serving, stir in the peppercorns.
- Slice the parfait, or just scoop out, and serve with the garnish.

Wine note

Either serve a sweetish wine like a German Spätlese or a crisp Pinot Blanc from Alsace.

SUMMER

Salad of Artichokes, Quail's Eggs and Pecorino

This rather unlikely combination was the result of a happy accident, when a shooting party decided to stay on for supper before setting out home. The fridge was rather bare except for these principle ingredients, so a little inspiration was needed. You can make this look really pretty, and it's worth spending a little time over it. Soup plates would be a splendid way of framing the attractive shapes.

Serves 6
Preparation time: 40 minutes

12 quail's eggs
1 head frisée, trimmed and divided into leaves
3 tablespoons walnut oil
large pinch of flaked Maldon sea salt
6 large globe artichokes, prepared (see Loin of Lamb with Artichokes, page 142)
150g (5½oz) pecorino, shaved with a peeler *or* cut into thin slices

- Put the quail's eggs in cold water and bring to the boil. Boil for 3 minutes, then drain, refresh and peel. (If the quail's eggs are to be served whole, cook for 2 minutes 15 seconds.) Halve the eggs lengthways and reserve.
- Mix the frisée with the oil and salt. Divide among the plates. Garnish each plate with a whole or quartered artichoke and 2 halved eggs. Arrange the shaved pecorino on top and serve with crusty bread.

Chef's tip
Disposable rubber gloves are very useful for tasks such as peeling artichokes or filleting fish.

Summer

Watermelon, Chicory and Feta Salad

This is a fantastic salad, ideal for summer eating, inspired by the brilliant Peter Gordon of the Sugar Club restaurant in London. The mixture of sweet and salty flavours reminds me of the Middle East and its very refreshing cuisine – the best thing to consume in Syria is a pomegranate juice on the street as you stroll along, followed by a falafel with tangy sauce. This follows that wonderful tradition.

Serves 6
Preparation time: 30 minutes

500g (1lb 2oz) watermelon flesh, cut into slices and seeded
2 heads chicory, separated into leaves
250g (9oz) feta, cut into slices
50g (scant 2oz) pumpkin seeds
1 teaspoon olive oil
4 spring onions, greens only, sliced

For the rocket pesto
50g (scant 2oz) rocket
50g (scant 2oz) pumpkin seeds
1 garlic clove, crushed
60ml (2floz) olive oil
salt and pepper

- Layer the sliced watermelon, chicory and feta in a serving dish and reserve.
- Toast the pumpkin seeds in the oil and season with salt. Scatter over the salad.
- Put the spring onion greens in a bowl of iced water and set aside.
- To make the pesto, combine the rocket, pumpkin seeds, garlic and oil in a blender or food processor and process until smooth. Season.
- Drizzle the rocket pesto over the salad and top with the curled spring onion greens.

Autumn

Pad Thai

Pad Thai, which simply means Thai noodles, has been elevated to the national dish of that country. A typical example of peasant cuisine, it is cheap and filling yet quite delicious. Preserved radish is white radish (mooli or daikon) which has been salted and then dried. It is easily bought from Thai supermarkets in vacuum packs (often confusingly labelled preserved turnip). It has a distinctive flavour. I can think of no substitute, although cubed fresh shiitake mushrooms come closest in texture. If you use mushrooms instead, a pinch of extra seasoning may be appropriate as the radish is quite salty.

Serves 2
Preparation time: 10 minutes
Cooking time: 5 minutes

4 tablespoons sunflower oil
2 garlic cloves, finely chopped
1 egg
115g (4oz) Chinese egg noodles, soaked in water until soft then drained
2 tablespoons lemon juice
1½ tablespoons fish sauce
½ teaspoon sugar
2 tablespoons chopped roasted cashews
½ teaspoon chilli powder
1 tablespoon finely chopped preserved radish (see above)
30g (1oz) bean sprouts
2 spring onions, chopped into 2.5cm (1in) pieces
1 sprig of fresh coriander, coarsely chopped
lemon wedges to garnish

- Heat the oil in a wok or frying pan, add the garlic and fry until golden brown. Break the egg into the wok, stir quickly and cook for a couple of seconds. Then add the noodles and stir well, scraping down the sides of the wok to ensure they mix with the garlic and egg.
- One after the other, add the lemon juice, fish sauce, sugar, half the cashews, the chilli powder, the preserved radish, 1 tablespoon of the bean sprouts and the spring onions, stirring quickly all the time.

- Test the noodles for tenderness. When done, turn on to a serving plate. Arrange the remaining cashews and bean sprouts around the dish. Garnish with the coriander and lemon wedges and serve.

Wine note

Serve with a citron pressé *or a Chablis.*

Autumn

Antipasto with Pickled Aubergines and Stromboli

There are few better places to construct a picnic from than a deli in Italy. The combination of cured meats, bread and pickles, with a few fresh tomatoes and some fruit, is sheer bliss. The quantities and varieties of meat are entirely up to you, but these aubergines and the bread are really special. The aubergine recipe is a version of one made by my godson's great uncle, David, a great gardener, pickler and scrimper! Stromboli is so named for the way the cheese exudes, like lava from the volcano.

Serves 8
Preparation time (aubergines): 30 minutes plus 2 months maturing
Preparation time (Stromboli): 1¼ hours
Cooking time (Stromboli): 30–35 minutes

For the aubergines
2 aubergines, about 500g (1lb 2oz) total, sliced into rounds
150ml (5floz) olive oil
250ml (8½floz) white wine vinegar
125g (4½oz) caster sugar
1 teaspoon salt
a 2cm (¾in) piece of peeled fresh ginger
12 black peppercorns
1 tablespoon yellow mustard seeds
a 4cm (1½in) piece of cinnamon stick

For the Stromboli
1 quantity of risen Focaccia dough (see page 233)
280g (10oz) mozzarella, roughly chopped
4 handfuls of fresh basil leaves
2 tablespoons olive oil
125g (4½oz) provolone cheese, cut into 1cm (½in) cubes
85g (3oz) Parma ham, each slice torn into 5–6 pieces
¼–½ teaspoon coarse sea salt
20 sprigs of fresh rosemary
extra virgin olive oil for drizzling

- To prepare the aubergines, sprinkle the slices with salt and leave to drain for 20 minutes. Rinse, drain and dry. Fry the aubergine slices in 4 tablespoons of the

- olive oil until golden brown on both sides. Drain on kitchen paper. Pack the slices into a sterilized 500ml (17floz) Kilner jar.
- Bring the vinegar to the boil with the sugar and salt. Pack the spices along the sides of the jar and pour in the vinegar to fill almost to the top. Add the remaining oil to seal the surface, and close the jar. Keep in a cool, dry, dark place for 2 months before serving.
- For the Stromboli, roll out the dough to a 33 × 28cm (13 × 11in) rectangle, about 5mm–1cm (¼–½in) thick. Sprinkle over the mozzarella and basil leaves, then drizzle over half the olive oil. Top evenly with the provolone and the Parma ham. Roll up like a Swiss roll, from a long side, and tuck in the ends.
- Lay the roll on an oiled baking sheet with the join underneath. Cover with a cloth or cling film and leave for 10 minutes. (The dough will not rise much at this stage.) Meanwhile, preheat the oven to 200°C/400°F/Gas 6.
- Remove the cover and pierce the roll all over with a large two-pronged meat fork, through to the baking sheet. Lightly brush the surface with the remaining olive oil and sprinkle over the sea salt. Tuck the rosemary sprigs into the surface of the dough. Bake for 30–35 minutes or until cooked through and pale golden. Drizzle over a little extra virgin olive oil and transfer to a wire rack to cool.

Wine note

Most wine tastes great outdoors, as do beers. My choice would be a powerful red like a cheap Shiraz chilled to quite a low temperature.

Autumn

Roast Squash Soup and Parmesan Wafers

As an impecunious student in Auckland in the late 1980s, pumpkin soup was rather a staple to my flatmates and me, although it tended to be made with beer, melted cheese and chilli, and was served with fresh home-made scones and more beer. Aah, such days! I've refined the recipe, so it's just as yummy now, and have left out the hangovers and squalid digs.

Serves 6
Preparation time: 1 hour 35 minutes
Cooking time: 30 minutes

1 large kabocha squash, weighing about 1.5kg (3lb 3oz)
100g (3½oz) butter
100g (3½oz) Parmesan, freshly grated
2 large onions, thinly sliced
3 tablespoons olive oil
4 garlic cloves, chopped
1.5 litres (2¾ pints) chicken stock
½ teaspoon freshly grated nutmeg
250 ml (8½floz) crème fraîche
12 fresh chives
salt and black pepper

- Preheat the oven to 180°C/350°F/Gas 4.
- Halve the squash horizontally and remove the seeds and fibres. Season well with black pepper and divide the butter between the two halves. Roast for 1½ hours. Then roughly chop into 2cm (¾in) pieces, with the skin.
- While the squash is roasting, make 6 piles of the Parmesan on greased or non-stick oven trays, about 10cm (4in) apart. Bake in the same oven for 10 minutes or so until melted, browned and yummy. These can be left flat or curled over ramekins or such-like while still warm. Leave to cool.
- In a large saucepan, fry the sliced onions in the olive oil until softened. Add the garlic and continue frying for another minute or so, then add the squash and the stock. Season with the nutmeg, salt and pepper. Bring to the boil, then simmer for 20 minutes.

- Ladle the mixture into a blender or food processor and blend until smooth. Reheat if necessary and check the seasoning. Serve hot, topped with crème fraîche and whole chives, with the Parmesan wafers.

> ### Chef's tip
> *When choosing vegetables and melons, always buy the ones that seem heavy for their size, because they will have better texture and be fresher.*

Autumn

Porcini Risotto

Risotto is the most versatile of dishes, making good use of all manner of ingredients, especially rare or expensive ones such as saffron, asparagus and wild mushrooms. It's also easy to stretch if you don't know how many are coming for supper! It is essential to use risotto rice, rather than long-grain. Long-grain rice is normally washed before cooking to remove excess starch grains, which make it go 'claggy'; however, risotto rice is never washed as the starch is an essential component of the dish – it dissolves in the stock to produce the characteristic creaminess. Risotto, once mastered, will become a staple in your kitchen as it is in mine. Good stock and a patient stirring hand are all that's needed to make a satisfying meal. When done, the risotto should be all'onda, or 'of the wave' – when spooned into bowls, it shouldn't immediately spread out but should gradually lose its shape. The texture should be creamy and the rice grains firm but not chalky.

Serves 8
Preparation time: 15 minutes
Cooking time: about 30 minutes

100g (3½oz) pancetta *or* smoked bacon, cut into large lardons
100g (3½oz) fresh porcini, sliced
1 medium onion, finely chopped
100g (3½oz) butter

450g (1lb) risotto rice
about 1.5 litres (2¾ pints) chicken stock *or* water, heated to boiling
200g (7oz) Parmesan, freshly grated

- Fry the pancetta or bacon, mushrooms and onion in half the butter until the onion is soft.
- Add the rice and continue frying for 2 minutes, stirring.
- Gradually add the boiling stock to the pan, a ladleful at a time, stirring; wait for each portion of stock to be almost all absorbed before adding the next. The total cooking time will be about 20 minutes.
- Stir in the rest of the butter and the Parmesan. Serve soon!

Other flavours
Beetroot Risotto: This has an amazing colour! Omit the porcini, and add 4 cooked beetroot, peeled and puréed, with the butter and Parmesan.

Fish or Seafood Risotto: Omit the pancetta, porcini and Parmesan, and use fish stock and white wine instead of the chicken stock. Add chunks of fish or seafood of your choice towards the end of the cooking time.

Saffron Risotto (Milanese): Dissolve a pinch of saffron threads in the stock and omit the porcini.

Wine note

The rich porcini flavour would be perfectly partnered by the wonderful flavours of a Brunello.

Autumn

Rabbit and Shiitake Terrine

Rabbit is sadly overlooked in Britain, which is a shame as it is wonderfully versatile. This dish balances the rather gentle flavour of rabbit fillets with earthy lentils and mushrooms. Leaves of gelatine are now widely available and just need to be briefly soaked before use.

Serves 10
Preparation time: 15 minutes
Cooking time: 30 minutes

250g (9oz) Puy lentils
1 onion
45g (1½oz) dried shiitake mushrooms
the saddles from 4 wild rabbits (keep the legs for another dish)
2 tablespoons olive oil

250ml (8½floz) clear chicken stock
4 gelatine leaves, soaked in water to soften then drained
8 Savoy cabbage leaves, blanched for 1 minute and refreshed
Basic Vinaigrette (see page 229) to serve

- Cook the lentils with the peeled onion in boiling unsalted water for 20 minutes. Drain, rinse and reserve. Discard the onion.
- Meanwhile, soak the mushrooms in boiling water for 10 minutes. Drain, squeezing out excess water, then cut off the stalks which are always tough. Slice the mushrooms.
- Preheat the oven to 220°C/425°F/Gas 7.
- Brown the saddles from the rabbits in the oil, then transfer to the oven. Roast for 12 minutes. Remove from the oven and leave to rest for 5 minutes. Carve the whole fillets from the bones.
- Heat the stock and dissolve the gelatine in it. Set aside.
- Line a 25cm (10in) long loaf tin with cling film. Line the tin with the cabbage leaves, leaving enough to cover the top when filled. Make a layer of lentils on the bottom of the tin, then lay 2 rabbit fillets on top. Scatter over some mushrooms. Repeat the layers. Alternatively, rather than making layers form the ingredients into a mosaic pattern.
- When all the ingredients are in the tin, pour in the stock mixture and tap the tin on the work surface a couple of times to dispel any air bubbles. Cover with the

reserved cabbage leaves and more cling film. Place weights on top and refrigerate overnight.
- To serve, cut into 2cm (¾in) slices and serve with the vinaigrette, salad and bread.

Wine note

A rich white Burgundy or a light Australian Chardonnay will complement the rabbit and lentils.

Autumn

Parsnip and Porcini Soup with Mustard and Chive Sabayon

Here is another use for the porcini or cep mushroom, the most wonderful of all of autumn's gifts. The musty scent and intense flavour lift the humble parsnip into another level altogether. The sabayon can be omitted, but is a very special addition.

Serves 8–10
Preparation time: 20 minutes
Cooking time: 35 minutes

For the soup
45g (1½oz) dried porcini
3 tablespoons extra virgin olive oil
300g (10½oz) onions, finely chopped
3 garlic cloves, finely chopped
800g (1¾lb) parsnips, peeled, cored and diced
1 litre (1¾ pints) chicken stock *or* water
600 ml (1 pint) double cream
salt and pepper

For the sabayon
2 egg yolks
1 tablespoon dry white wine
1 tablespoon grain mustard
15g (½oz) fresh chives, snipped into 1cm (½in) lengths

- Soak the dried porcini in 500ml (17floz) of boiling water for 20 minutes, drain, reserving the soaking water. Strain the water through a piece of kitchen paper and set aside.
- Heat the olive oil in a saucepan, add the onions and season with salt and pepper. When the onions are translucent but not coloured, add the garlic and continue to cook for 1 minute.
- Add the parsnips, chicken stock, the porcini soaking water and the porcini. Simmer gently for 30 minutes.

- Purée in a blender or food processor. Stir through the double cream and reheat if necessary. Check the seasoning. (The soup can be kept at this stage or served immediately.)
- To make the sabayon, whisk the egg yolks with the wine in a large bowl set over a pan of boiling water. When the mixture is light and fluffy, remove from the heat and gently fold in the mustard and chives. The sabayon should remain fluffy.
- Pour a little sabayon into the centre of each bowl of soup and eat immediately.

Wine note

A heavy, perfumed white Rhône wine would be perfect with this.

Autumn

Warm Salad of Black Pudding and Apples

A great favourite of mine, black pudding works well with bland or delicate flavours as well as with those that are sharp. For example, sweet scallops and rich black pudding was a great fashion in the mid 1990s; the black and white pairing was also very striking. This is a very simple dish which could be elevated by a poached egg on top of each plate. A little fried bacon would make a starter version.

Serves 6
Preparation time: 12 minutes
Cooking time: 10 minutes

18 slices black pudding, each 1cm (½in) thick, stripped of wrappings, *or* the same amount cut into 1cm (½in) cubes
2 tablespoons sunflower oil (optional)
1 green apple, such as Granny Smith
1 sweet red apple, such as Fuji
1 head frisée, trimmed of coarse leaves

For the dressing
5 tablespoons olive oil
1 tablespoon cider vinegar
1 tablespoon grain mustard
salt and pepper

- Gently fry the black pudding in the sunflower oil, or grill.
- Meanwhile, whisk the oil, vinegar and mustard together in a large bowl and season.
- Core the apples and slice directly into the dressing. Toss to coat. (The acid in the vinegar will prevent the apples from discolouring.) Add the frisée and toss to dress thoroughly. Divide among 6 plates, forming into attractive piles.
- When the black pudding has been fried or grilled to a pleasantly browned stage, drain away any excess fat and place on top of the salad. Serve immediately with crusty bread.

Autumn

Chicory, Aubergine and Goat's Cheese Gratin

This is ideal for a starter or a light supper. Originally a French dish made with slices of cooked ham and a blue cheese sauce, to slightly modernize it I've replaced the ham with cooked slices of aubergine. This then can fit into a vegetarian or kosher meal and is no less delicious!

Serves 6
Preparation time: 55 minutes
Cooking time: 30 minutes

1 long aubergine, cut lengthways into 6 slices, each 5mm (¼in) thick
360ml (12floz) white wine
6 heads chicory, trimmed of any wilted leaves
60ml (2floz) olive oil
500ml (17floz) whole milk
15g (½oz) butter
30g (1oz) plain flour
¼ teaspoon freshly grated nutmeg
3 tablespoons freshly grated Parmesan
150g (5½oz) soft goat's cheese, mild or strong, to your taste
salt and pepper

- Sprinkle the aubergine slices with salt and leave to drain for 30 minutes. Rinse, drain and dry.
- Make the wine up to 1 litre (1 ¾ pints) with hot water and season. Poach the chicory heads in this mixture for 10–12 minutes or until almost tender. Drain and reserve.
- Fry the aubergine slices in the olive oil until just past golden brown; drain on kitchen paper and reserve.
- Make a béchamel sauce with the milk, butter and flour (see page 00) and season with the nutmeg, salt and pepper.
- Preheat the oven to 180°C/350°F/Gas 4.
- Butter an ovenproof dish large enough to take all the chicory in one layer and dust with half the Parmesan. Spread each of the aubergine slices with the goat's

cheese and wrap around a head of chicory, then place in the dish, with the join underneath to keep from unrolling. Cover with the béchamel sauce and sprinkle the remaining Parmesan over the top. Bake for 30 minutes or until well browned and bubbling.

> ## Wine note
> *The creamy, cheesey sauce suggests a clean white such as a Muscadet or Chablis.*

Winter

Sprout and Chestnut Soup with Truffle Oil

Brussels sprouts are really my bête noir *and will always haunt my Christmases. However, this soup is the one way I can imagine eating huge quantities of our Belgian friends (although the consequences would be unimaginable, the flavour is superb). Truffle oil is always in my cupboard as it lifts the humblest of dishes into nectar. The aroma is unparalleled, but is easily overpowering – just a few drops per person is more than enough.*

Serves 8
Preparation time: 30 minutes
Cooking time: 15 minutes

1 kg (2¼lb) Brussels sprouts, trimmed and halved	2 litres (3½ pints) chicken stock
50g (scant 2oz) butter	300ml (10floz) double cream
250g (9oz) vacuum-packed chestnuts	2 teaspoons truffle oil
	salt and pepper

- Fry the sprouts very gently in the butter until brown, seasoning with salt and pepper. Add the chestnuts and stock and simmer for 10 minutes.
- Purée in a blender or food processor and stir in the cream. Reheat gently if necessary.
- Garnish each bowl with three or four drops of truffle oil and serve.

Winter

Lobster Bisque

The sexiest of all soups, this has splendid aphrodisiac qualities, especially when garnished with truffle oil (you'll just have to take my word for its efficacy!). Once the lobster is just a memory the shells can be rinsed and frozen or used straight away. In fact, for a special picnic, the cold lobster meat can be used for the main course and the soup taken in a thermos flask.

Serves 8
Preparation time: 30 minutes
Cooking time: 1 hour

the shells of 4 lobsters
100ml (3½floz) olive oil
1 small onion, diced
1 small carrot, diced
3 outer layers of bulb fennel, diced
1 garlic clove, crushed
1 sprig of fresh thyme
1 sprig of young fresh tarragon

100ml (3½floz) cognac
100ml (3½floz) Madeira
200ml (7floz) dry white wine
6 ripe tomatoes, diced
1 teaspoon tomato purée
100ml (3½floz) whipping cream
salt and pepper

- Sear the lobster shells in the hot olive oil for 1 minute, then add the vegetables, garlic and herbs. Sweat over a low heat for a few minutes.
- Spoon out the excess oil from the pan, then deglaze with the cognac and Madeira. Reduce to one-quarter of the original volume.
- Add the wine, tomatoes and tomato purée, then 2.5 litres (4⅓ pints) water. Bring to the boil, skimming well. Simmer for 25 minutes.
- Strain the solids, reserving the liquid, and process them in a blender or food processor. Return to the pan through a sieve. Add the reserved liquid. Simmer, skimming, to reduce by one-third.
- Add the cream and season. Serve hot.

Winter

Shallot Tarts with Sage Cream

If ever I was stranded on a desert island and rescued after a substantial period of time, I would head straight for the splendiferous George Hotel in Stamford, Lincplnshire. There Chris Pitman and his inestimable wife Mary serve great, hearty food, with delicate touches much like these tarts. I can think of few ways of spending a Sunday that could compete with a yomp around the park at Burghley House, and then repairing to a roast partridge at the George.

Serves 6
Preparation time: 40 minutes
Cooking time: 10 minutes

15g (½oz) fresh sage leaves
125ml (4½floz) double cream
72 small shallots, peeled
5 teaspoons olive oil
2 teaspoons fresh thyme leaves

350g (12½oz) ready-rolled puff pastry
oil for deep-frying
salt and pepper
truffle oil to serve

- Preheat the oven to 200°C/400°F/Gas 6.
- Reserve 6 nice sage leaves and add the rest to the cream. Bring to the boil, then remove from the heat and leave to go cold so the sage flavour can infuse the cream.
- Roll the shallots in the oil, season and roast for about 10 minutes or until well coloured and soft. Leave the oven on.
- Grease six 10cm (4in) non-stick tartlet tins. Arrange the shallots attractively in the tins. Season and sprinkle with the thyme leaves.
- Cut 6 circles of puff pastry, just larger than the tins, and cover each one, pressing down well. Make a small hole in the centre of each pastry lid. Bake in the preheated oven for 10 minutes or until well browned.

STARTERS

- Meanwhile, deep-fry the reserved sage leaves; drain on kitchen paper and reserve.
- Strain the sage-infused cream, then whip to a soft peak.
- Turn out the tarts, drizzle with a little truffle oil and top each with a neat spoonful of the cream. Use the deep-fried sage leaves like flags to finish. Serve hot.

Wine note
Try a white Rioja.

FISH

Spring

Saffron Broth of Mussels and Spring Herbs

I first made this dish on Masterchef in 1993, the beginning of my cooking on TV. It is borrowed from Georges Blanc, a brilliant French chef working in the 'Cuisine Mincer', or healthy, style, avoiding red meat, cream or butter. The fragrance of the saffron and richness of the mussels works really well. Saffron is one of my favourite spices (the other being cumin). It was once worth its weight in gold. In medieval times saffron was grown in Britain, notably Essex (in Saffron Walden) and Cornwall, where it is still used in saffron loaf. The best saffron now comes from La Mancha in Spain. Always buy whole stamens or 'thread' saffron as powdered may be adulterated. The cheap saffron offered to tourists abroad is often safflower and has no flavour.

Serves 8
Preparation time: 20 minutes
Cooking time: 30 minutes

12 shallots, finely chopped
200ml (7floz) olive oil
1 teaspoon tomato purée
2 garlic cloves, finely chopped
1kg (2¼lb) mussels, scrubbed and cleaned
3 sticks lemon grass
2 bay leaves
20g (½oz) butter
pinch of saffron threads
2 teaspoons mixed fresh herb leaves (tarragon, chervil, chives, basil and dill)
2 handfuls of chopped vegetables (I use 2 courgettes, 1 aubergine, 1 potato and 3 tomatoes cut into diamonds measuring 1cm x 5mm/½ x ¼in)
2 teaspoons crème fraîche

- Gently sweat the shallots in 1 teaspoon of the olive oil in a saucepan until soft. Add the tomato purée and the garlic, stir and cook for a further 2 minutes.
- Meanwhile, steam the mussels until the shells open. Discard any that do not open. Remove them from their shells, and filter the liquor that will have been

released through kitchen paper. Make the liquor up to 1.5 litres (2 ¾ pints) with water and add to the shallots. Set the mussels aside.
- Smash the lemon grass and add with the bay leaves to the mussel broth. Boil for 10 minutes, then strain. Whisk in the butter. Add the saffron and herbs. Keep warm.
- Fry the vegetables in the remaining olive oil until they start to brown lightly, then drain.
- Place the mussels and vegetables in a tureen and pour the broth over the top. Stir in the crème fraîche and serve immediately.

Wine note

A crisp Muscadet or a well-chilled white Rhône will be perfect with this.

Spring

Turbot with Peas, Broad Beans and Asparagus

Turbot is, without doubt, the king of fishes, and a finer meal could not be had than simply grilled turbot with salad and chips. This is a slightly more polite version of that idea and I highly recommend it. Turbot is not cheap, but is a worthwhile treat. Pieces of fillet from larger fish are thicker and therefore more succulent.

Serves 6
Preparation time: 10 minutes
Cooking time: 20 minutes

140g (5oz) shelled fresh *or* frozen peas
200g (7oz) asparagus tips
6 pieces of turbot fillet, each about 170g (6oz)
700ml (1 pint 3½floz) fish stock
4 shallots, finely chopped
30g (1oz) butter
100ml (3½floz) double cream
115g (4oz) frozen broad beans, thawed and skinned
2 tablespoons chopped fresh chervil
pepper
6 sprigs of fresh chervil

- Blanch fresh peas in boiling salted water for 1 minute; drain and refresh. Thaw frozen peas. Blanch the asparagus in boiling salted water for 2 minutes; drain and refresh. Set aside.
- Poach the turbot in the fish stock for about 7 minutes or until just done.
- Meanwhile, sauté the shallots in the butter to soften but not to colour. Draw 100ml (3½floz) of the fish stock from the fish, add to the shallots and reduce by two-thirds. Add the cream and reduce by half. Season with pepper and stir through the beans and chopped chervil. Heat briefly. The sauce is now ready and must be used immediately or the chervil will discolour.
- Remove the turbot steaks from the stock and drain well. Serve on a platter with the sauce poured over and the vegetables strewn round. Garnish with the sprigs of chervil.

SPRING

Tortellini of Crab with Chervil Butter Sauce

Chervil really is the herb best suited to delicate fish flavours, and this dish shows that very well. Crab can be bought canned or frozen, but is really at its finest when fresh. I wouldn't suggest you should cook and pick your own crab as it is far too tedious for words, so bless the good people who do it for us. Rather than buying the crab in a supermarket, I suggest that you seek out a good local fishmonger.

Serves 8
Preparation time: 1 hour
Cooking time: 10 minutes

Basic Pasta Dough (see page 232)

For the filling
150g (5½oz) fresh white crab meat
150g (5½oz) ricotta
1 tablespoon chopped fresh chervil
white pepper

For the chervil butter sauce
juice of 1 lemon
250g (9oz) butter, cut into small pieces
2 tablespoons chopped fresh chervil
8 bunches of fresh chervil to garnish

- Mix the crab meat and ricotta together with the chopped chervil and season with white pepper.
- Cut the sheets of pasta dough into 32 circles, each 10cm (4in) in diameter. Working swiftly, place a teaspoon of the crab filling on one side of each circle. (Do not be tempted to overfill the tortellini or they might pop as they cook because the filling will expand.) Brush the rim of each circle with water and fold over into a half-moon shape, pressing to seal the edges.
- To shape the tortellini, bring the two pointed ends of the straight edge of each half-moon around your index finger and press well to seal. Bring the rim up and around the bulk of the parcel to form the brim of the 'hat', making sure there are no rips or tears.

- Cook the tortellini in lots of boiling salted water for 3 minutes, then drain. (You can prepare the tortellini ahead of time, in which case cook for only 2 minutes, then drain and refresh; reheat later in a little water and butter.)
- While the tortellini is cooking, make the butter sauce. Heat the lemon juice with the same quantity of water in a small saucepan, then slowly whisk in the butter over a very low heat. The lemon juice should emulsify very easily with the butter as long as the heat is not too high. Fold in the chervil, dress the pasta and serve, garnished with bunches of chervil.

Spring

Crab Risotto with Coconut Milk and Coriander

This risotto is an idea I had whilst thinking about fusion cuisine and shows that almost no dish is exempt from tinkering. In this Asian version, part of the oil and stock have been replaced by coconut milk. It is essential to use risotto rice, rather than long-grain.

Serves 8
Preparation time: 10 minutes
Cooking time: 25 minutes

1 medium onion, finely chopped
3 garlic cloves, finely chopped
3 tablespoons sunflower oil
450g (1lb) risotto rice
about 1 litre (1¾ pints) fish stock *or* water, heated to boiling

400ml (14floz) coconut milk
5 fresh lime leaves, finely shredded
250g (9oz) white crab meat
15g (½oz) fresh coriander, chopped
black pepper

- Fry the onion and garlic in the oil until soft. Add the rice and fry for a further 2 minutes, stirring. Slowly add the boiling stock, a ladleful at a time, cooking for about 10 minutes. Let each addition be absorbed before adding the next. Then gradually add the coconut milk in the same way. Cook until the grains of rice are still firm but not chalky, using as much coconut milk as possible and then more fish stock if necessary.
- When the rice is almost done, stir through the lime leaves, crab meat and coriander. Season well with plenty of black pepper. The finished risotto should be reasonably fluid.

SPRING

Glazed Smoked Haddock with Mustard Cream

Smoked haddock is such a joy that it is almost incredible to me that restaurants don't serve it more frequently. It is usually poached in milk and thus done makes a splendid risotto. The smoky flavour also seems to work well with grain mustard. Always buy the best finnan haddock, which is undyed and has a far finer flavour than other smoked haddock.

Serves 6
Preparation time: 5 minutes
Cooking time: 50 minutes

a 1.5kg (3lb 3oz) whole undyed smoked haddock
500ml (17floz) whole milk
25g (scant 1oz) butter
25g (scant 1oz) plain flour
2 tablespoons grain mustard
2 tablespoons chopped parsley
100g (3½oz) fresh white breadcrumbs
55g (2oz) Cheddar cheese, grated

- Preheat the grill, or preheat the oven to 190°C/375°F/Gas 5.
- Skin and bone the haddock, keeping the flesh in as big pieces as possible. Poach very gently in the milk for about 12 minutes or until done. Remove from the milk in large pieces and keep warm.
- Make a béchamel sauce with the butter, flour and milk used to poach the fish (see page 228). The resulting sauce will be much thinner than a normal béchamel. Add the grain mustard and the parsley.
- Place the fish in a gratin dish that will hold it comfortably and cover with the mustard sauce. Mix together the breadcrumbs and cheese and sprinkle over the surface. Grill for 15 minutes, or bake for 30 minutes, or until a golden brown crust has formed. A perfect supper.

Spring

Smoked Fish Terrine and Samphire Salad

Smoking is an ancient means of preserving food and, as with salt beef and retsina, the flavour has become an end in itself. Britain abounds with fantastic smoked (and fresh!) fish, and this recipe uses it to great effect. The dish is very rich, though, so only the smallest portions are neccessary. The samphire salad serves as a seasonal garnish to cut through the richness; if samphire isn't available, just drizzle the slices of terrine with walnut oil before serving. This is an ideal dish to make when you are busy.

Serves 10
Preparation time: 30 minutes
Chilling time: 12–36 hours

For the terrine
1 smoked trout
340g (12oz) smoked haddock fillets
340g (12oz) smoked eel fillets
400g (14oz) smoked salmon slices
200g (7oz) mascarpone
85g (3oz) rocket *or* watercress
1 teaspoon lemon juice
salt and pepper

For the salad
400g (14oz) fresh samphire
2½ tablespoons walnut oil

- Remove all skin and bones from the trout, haddock and eel. Trim so that there are 2 batons of each kind of fish about 23cm (9in) long.
- Line a 23cm (9in) long loaf tin with cling film, then line with the salmon slices, to leave an overhang of salmon and cling film on each side long enough to fold over the top of the terrine later.
- Purée the mascarpone with the rocket and lemon juice in a blender or food processor until almost smooth. Season with salt and pepper.
- Spread a 5mm (¼in) layer of mascarpone mousse over the bottom of the salmon-lined tin. Lay the haddock fillets side by side on top and cover thinly with more mousse. Make sure that the mousse goes between the two fillets.

Repeat with the trout and then with the eel, covering with the last scraping of mousse.
- Fold the slices of salmon over the top to finish neatly and then fold over the cling film. Weight down. Chill for 12–36 hours.
- For the salad, wash and pick over the samphire. Dress with the walnut oil and a little freshly ground black pepper.
- To serve, unwrap the cling film from the top of the terrine and invert on to a chopping board. Lift off the tin and cling film in one. Cut into 2cm (¾in) slices. Serve with the samphire salad and lots of crusty bread.

Wine note

The richness of the mascarpone and the oiliness of the smoked fish suggest a full-bodied Meursault or another, better, white Burgundy.

SUMMER

Chargrilled Tuna Loin with Salsa Verde and Tapenade

I served this dish as a fish course to Rachel Cook of The Sunday Times. *Her review led to a huge upsurge in my popularity, and the dish has been a firm favourite ever since. It's important to use really fresh tuna, and to grill it just to medium rare so that the flesh remains moist – think of it as the best steak (if you prefer steak well done, try another dish). The Pommes Anna are not essential, but add a really nice contrast to the meatiness of the tuna.*

Serves 6
Preparation time: 1 hour 10 minutes
Cooking time: 20 minutes

6 tuna loin steaks, as fresh as possible
olive oil
salt and pepper
1 tablespoon Sichuan peppercorns to garnish

For the pommes Anna
3 large *or* 6 small potatoes, about 500g (1lb 2oz), peeled and thinly sliced
100g (3½oz) butter, melted

For the tapenade
100g (3½oz) dry-cured black olives, stoned
2 anchovy fillets
45g (1½oz) fresh flat-leaf parsley, stalks discarded
1 tablespoon olive oil

For the salsa verde
50g (scant 2oz) fresh coriander, stalks discarded
50g (scant 2oz) fresh flat-leaf parsley, stalks discarded
2 garlic cloves, crushed
2 tablespoons capers, drained, rinsed and dried
1 tablespoon green peppercorns packed in brine, drained
2 anchovy fillets
3 tablespoons olive oil
1 tablespoon white wine vinegar

- Preheat the oven to 200°C/400°F/Gas 6.
- Trim any dark muscle from the tuna steaks, and try to make them a reasonably uniform size. Douse them with a little olive oil on both sides and set aside.
- To make the pommes Anna, rinse the potato slices in cold water, then drain and dry on a tea cloth or kitchen paper. Brush six 10cm (4in) diameter non-stick tins with melted butter. Arrange the potato slices in the tins, in rings in 3–4 layers, brushing each layer with melted butter and seasoning with pepper. Bake for about 20 minutes or until the tops have browned attractively.
- Meanwhile, make the tapenade by combining all the ingredients in a blender and blending until quite smooth. Scrape out into a bowl and set aside. Wash the blender, then put in all the ingredients for the salsa verde and blend to a thickish sauce/paste (do not do this too far in advance or the salsa verde will lose its vibrant verdancy). Set aside.
- When the pommes Anna are ready, turn them out on to a baking sheet. Keep warm.
- Char-grill the tuna steaks on a very hot ridged cast-iron grill pan for about 4 minutes on each side, depending on the thickness of the steaks and your taste (tuna cooked medium or beyond will be dry).
- To serve, place the pommes Anna on individual plates and set the tuna steaks on top. Add a drizzle of salsa verde, a sprinkling of Sichuan peppercorns and a *quenelle* or spoonful of tapenade to each steak.

SUMMER

BOUILLABAISE WITH ROUILLE

The Mediterranean abounds with mixed fish stews like this one, which were created to use the daily catch, fishing not being the exact science that fish farming is – you know what the harvest will be when you plant a row of carrots, but casting a net always brings in a surprise. Ideally, use a variety of fish offering different textures and colours. Monkfish and red mullet are particularly good, as are raw prawns, langoustines and mussels. The rouille is an acquired taste, but I love hot stuff.

Serves 6
Preparation time: 35 minutes
Cooking time: 30 minutes

1 loaf French bread, cut into 1cm (½in) slices
1.8kg (4lb) mixed seafood to your taste
6 tablespoons olive oil
8 shallots *or* 1 medium onion, finely chopped
2 tablespoons Pernod (optional)
2 garlic cloves, finely chopped (optional)
1kg (2¼lb) tomatoes, peeled and roughly chopped
600ml (1 pint) dry white wine *or* water

pinch of saffron threads
1 tablespoon finely chopped parsley
salt and pepper
grated Gruyère to serve

For the rouille
2 fresh red chillies, seeded
2 garlic cloves, finely chopped
1 slice white bread, crust removed
1 tablespoon white wine vinegar
200ml (7floz) sunflower *or* light olive oil

- Preheat the oven to 160°C/325°F/Gas 3.
- Lay the slices of bread on a baking tray and bake for about 30 minutes or until dry and crunchy but not coloured. When these croutons are ready, set them aside.
- Meanwhile, remove all skin and bones from the fish and cut into large chunks. Peel crustaceans such as prawns and langoustines. Leave molluscs such as mussels in their shells, but scrub well.
- Heat the olive oil in a large pan and fry the shallots (or onion) until translucent. Add the Pernod and garlic (if using) and the tomatoes with plenty

of seasoning. Stir over a high heat until the tomatoes are soft. Pour in the wine or water and bring to a simmer. Add the seafood, thickest kinds first and most delicate ones last, and simmer for about 10 minutes or until the thickest part of fish flakes easily. The idea is to cook the seafood thoroughly without it disintegrating.
- To make the rouille, grind the chillies and garlic with a pinch of coarse salt in a blender. Dip the bread into the soup to moisten it, then add to the blender with the vinegar and blend. Add the oil a little at a time, blending until the mixture thickens. If not serving immediately, keep covered with cling film.
- To serve, place a crouton in each of 6 bowls. Using a slotted spoon, lift the seafood out of the soup and arrange on the croutons. Stir the saffron and parsley into the soup and pour on to the seafood. Serve with the rest of the croutons, the rouille and Gruyère cheese.

Wine note

The traditional wine to serve with this dish is Muscadet.

Chargrilled Tuna Loin with Salsa Verde and Tapenade (page 71)

Hake in Serrano Ham with Capers and Saffron Pasta (page 89)

Roast Duck with Prune and Apple Stuffing (page 110)

Tarragon Chicken with Mushroom 'Boxes' (page 132)

Summer

Trout Fillet with Oregano Crust and Smoked Chilli Sauce

The smokiness of this dish and its ease of preparation make it most attractive. The sauce, made from chipotle chillies, is just wonderful, and is also perfect at breakfast with sausages, although the trouble is that it's a little too easy to eat too much and then suffer the consequences later.

Serve 4
Preparation time: 25 minutes
Cooking time: 1 hour

For the fish
4 trout fillets
1 tablespoon liquid smoke
65g (scant 2½oz) pecan pieces
50g (1¾oz) breadcrumbs
1 garlic clove, peeled
15g (½oz) fresh oregano, chopped
1 tablespoon olive oil

For the smoked chilli sauce
8 chipotle chillies, stalks and seeds removed
55g (2oz) finely sliced onions
90ml (3floz) cider vinegar
2 garlic cloves
4 tablespoons tomato ketchup
¼ teaspoon salt

- Skin the fish fillets, then marinate in the liquid smoke for 1–2 hours.
- To make the sauce, put all of the ingredients in a saucepan with 750ml (1¼ pints) water and simmer gently for 1 hour. Purée in a blender or food processor and set aside.
- Preheat the oven to 200°C/400°C/Gas 6.
- Combine the pecans, breadcrumbs, garlic, oregano and olive oil in a blender or food processor and blend to a wet crumb mixture.

- Fold the fillets over in half and place in a buttered oven tray. Press on the crumb mixture to make a crust and bake for 5 minutes.
- Drizzle the sauce over the fish and serve.

> ## Wine note
> *I serve an oaked New Zealand Chardonnay with this to balance the nuttiness of the crust on the fish.*

SUMMER

SUGAR-CURED SALMON, SWEET POTATO AND SAUTERNES SAUCE

Gravadlax is a very traditional Scandinavian dish, and this version takes the sweetness a step further. I developed this to illustrate the versatility of sugar for the Thai food series I made for Carlton Food Network. Although the three main elements in the recipe have sweetness, it isn't overwhelming. The steamed spinach adds colour and texture to the dish.

Serves 8
Preparation time: 25 minutes plus 24 hours resting
Cooking time: 15 minutes

a 600g (1lb 5oz) piece of salmon fillet
handful of coarse salt
handful of sugar
12 coriander seeds, crushed
4 tablespoons chopped fresh dill, plus more to garnish
1 large sweet potato, cut into ribbons on a mandolin
oil for deep-frying

For the sauce
2 shallots, finely chopped
30g (1oz) butter
250ml (8½floz) Sauternes *or* other sweet white wine
1 tablespoon vegetable stock
1 tablespoon double cream
salt and pepper

- Prepare the salmon, following the instructions for gravadlax (see Potato Blinis, Gravadlax and Citrus Basil Dressing, page 91), using the coriander seeds instead of the juniper berries.
- Brush and then wipe off the excess salt/sugar mixture. Cut the salmon fillet across into 8 thick slices. Set aside.

- To make the sauce, fry the shallots in the butter in a saucepan until softened. Add the Sauternes and reduce to about 4 tablespoons of liquid. Add the stock and mix well. Strain and whisk in the cream. Season with salt and pepper. Keep warm.
- Fry the salmon slices on a hot griddle or frying pan until browned on both sides but not cooked all the way through.
- Meanwhile, deep-fry the sweet potato ribbons in oil heated to 180°C/350°F to blanch, then drain and fry at 190°C/375°F or until a day-old cube of bread browns in 1 minute, until crisp and golden (just as you would fry chips). Drain on kitchen paper.
- Serve the salmon garnished with the sweet potato ribbons and dill and accompanied by the sauce.

Chef's tip

When re-using oil for deep-frying, strain it through a sieve lined with kitchen paper, then keep in the fridge. It is the small particles of food in the oil that make it go rancid much more quickly.

Summer

Salmon Steak with Sautéed Cucumbers and Mint

Salmon has become rather ubiquitous due to its farmed status – there are far too many corporate and cheaply catered events which rely on this poor overworked fish. But there is no reason why farmed salmon shouldn't be of the best quality. As long as the fish have to swim in a strong current, and are fed decent, well-flavoured food, they should have good-textured flesh with plenty of flavour. Whether farmed or wild, salmon is incredibly healthy, with its high concentrations of omega-3 oils. This dish takes the traditional accompaniments for salmon just a step further.

Serves 8
Preparation time: 10 minutes
Cooking time: 15 minutes

1 bottle cheap white wine
3 bay leaves
bunch of parsley stalks
12 black peppercorns
8 salmon steaks cut from a scaled fish

1 cucumber
50g (scant 2oz) butter
15g ($\frac{1}{2}$oz) fresh mint leaves, finely shredded

- Put the wine in a large wide pan with the same quantity of water, the bay leaves, parsley stalks and peppercorns. Bring to the boil. Poach the salmon steaks in the liquid for about 10 minutes.
- Meanwhile, peel the cucumber, cut it in half lengthways and remove the seeds. Take each half and halve again lengthways, then cut obliquely into 5mm ($\frac{1}{4}$in) slices. Sauté the slices, unseasoned, in the butter, adding the mint just before the cucumber turns transluscent.
- Drain the salmon steaks. Remove the skin by slipping the tine of a fork between the skin and flesh near the belly and winding upwards; the skin should just coil away from the flesh and can be discarded in one piece. Serve with the cucumbers and some fresh new potatoes

SUMMER

John Dory with Chicory and Tarragon Sabayon

John Dory is a flat fish with an enormous mouth and long fins. It is also known as St Peter's fish because it has two black spots, one on either flank, which are related to a story about it being fished out of the sea by the Saint. Underrated in Britain, the creamy flesh of this fish makes it well worth eating.

Serves 4
Preparation time: 5 minutes
Cooking time: 15 minutes

4 heads chicory
25g (scant 1oz) butter
50ml (2floz) white wine
4 boneless pieces of John Dory from a large fish
olive oil

2 egg yolks
1 teaspoon lemon juice
1 teaspoon chopped fresh tarragon, preferably baby leaves
salt and pepper

- Preheat the grill.
- Shred the chicory into 4–6 strips per leaf. Gently sauté in the butter until it starts to colour. Add the wine and cook gently until all the wine has evaporated. Season with salt and pepper and keep warm.
- Brush the fish with a little olive oil and season. Grill until just cooked, about 7 minutes.
- Meanwhile, put the egg yolks and lemon juice in a large glass bowl, set over a pan of boiling water and whisk until fluffy and creamy. Stir through the chopped tarragon.
- Serve each piece of fish on a pile of chicory and drizzle with the sabayon.

Autumn

Squid stuffed with its Tentacles and Prawns, Red Wine Sauce

Braised stuffed squid is a Masterchef dish and a frequent visitor to my dinner table. Most people find squid unappealing because of its rubber texture, which is a great sadness as tender squid is very easy to accomplish. Both very fast and very slow cooking will give tender results; this recipe uses the latter. The stuffed squid is browned quickly and then pot roasted over a very low light until tender. The original dish had three fillings and was served as a 'trio'. Being 1993 it was probably 'caressed by a symphony of coulis' as well, but thankfully we've all moved on! May I most firmly recommend you try this, and pass on anything caressed by a sauce!

Serves 6
Preparation time: 1 hour
Cooking time: 1 hour

6 squid with body sacs 15–20cm (6–8in) long
7–8 tablespoons olive oil
2 garlic cloves, finely chopped
2 tablespoons chopped parsley
100g (3½oz) peeled and seeded ripe tomato pulp
a little fresh red chilli
1 egg
20g (¾oz) fine dry breadcrumbs
2 red peppers
12 raw tiger or king prawns, peeled and deveined
170g (6oz) onions, very thinly sliced
100ml (3½floz) red wine
salt and pepper

- Clean the squid, and chop the fins and tentacles.
- Heat 4 tablespoons of the oil in a saucepan and sauté the garlic briefly. Add the parsley and chopped squid fins and tentacles and cook for 2 minutes. Add the tomato pulp and chilli and season with salt and pepper. Simmer with the lid

off for 30 minutes or until dryish. Leave to cool, then add the egg and breadcrumbs.
- While the stuffing mixture is simmering, roast and peel the peppers (see Roasted Pepper and Aubergine Terrine, page 36), then cut into 1cm (½in) strips.
- Stuff each squid body sac with a couple of strips of red pepper, 2 prawns and the tomato mixture. Do not overfill. Seal with wooden cocktail sticks and reserve.
- Heat the remaining oil in a wide pan and sauté the onions until softened. Raise the heat, add the stuffed squid and brown lightly all over. Add the wine and cover tightly. Braise for 45 minutes, adding a little water if necessary.
- To serve, slice the squid.

Autumn

Singaporean Lakhsa

Lakhsa, the national dish of Singapore, has become screamingly fashionable in Australia and New Zealand. The rich coconut-flavoured sauce and seafood is fleshed out by fresh egg noodles. A most satisfying supper dish to enjoy near a fire, thinking about the Asian sunshine and the beach.

Serves 6
Preparation time: 15 minutes
Cooking time: 20 minutes

2 fresh red chillies
4 garlic cloves, peeled
a 6cm (2½in) piece of fresh ginger, peeled and roughly chopped
1 teaspoon ground coriander
25g (scant 1oz) fresh coriander, roots, stems and leaves
50ml (2floz) toasted sesame oil
a 250g (9oz) piece of salmon fillet, skinned and sliced into 12 pieces
60ml (2floz) fresh lemon juice
1.2 litres (2 pints) coconut milk
800ml (1⅓ pints) fish *or* vegetable stock
60ml (2floz) fish sauce
12 king prawns, cooked, peeled and deveined
340g (12oz) fresh egg noodles
18 fresh mint leaves
3 spring onions, finely sliced

- Put the chillies, garlic, ginger, ground coriander, fresh coriander and sesame oil into a food processor and process to a coarse paste.
- Mix the salmon and lemon juice together and leave to marinate at room temperature while you make the lakhsa.
- Heat a large pot and add the spice paste. Fry for 1 minute, stirring well. Add the coconut milk and stock and bring to the boil. Simmer for 10 minutes, then add the fish sauce, prawns and the marinated salmon all at the same time. Stir gently for a few seconds.
- Warm the serving bowls. Divide the noodles among them and ladle on the soup. Sprinkle the mint and spring onions over the top and serve.

Autumn

Smoked Eel on Latkes with Rocket and Beetroot Relish

A modern version of an East End favourite, this dish pairs smoked eel (rather than salt beef) with latkes, the Eastern European/Jewish version of mash. Like rosti but yummier, latkes prove that any form of fried potatoes is a winner! Eel is not kosher and rocket is not East End, but the beetroot relish, chraim, is a perfect foil for all the other ingredients. This dish could almost be Thai in its balance of hot/cold, crunchy/soft and rich/acidic.

Serves 6
Preparation time: 45 minutes
Cooking time: 15 minutes

1 smoked eel, about 1kg (2¼lb), skinned and filleted
100g (3½oz) rocket
1 teaspoon walnut oil

For the latkes
1kg (2¼lb) baking potatoes, peeled and grated
250g (9oz) grated onion
150g (5½oz) plain flour
4 eggs

oil for deep-frying

For the beetroot relish
340g (12oz) fresh beetroot, cooked, peeled and grated
100g (3½oz) fresh horseradish, peeled and grated
100ml (3½oz) cider vinegar
1 teaspoon sugar
salt and pepper

- To make the relish, mix together the beetroot, horseradish, vinegar and sugar. Keep in a jar in the fridge for up to 1 week.
- For the latkes, wash the grated potato in two changes of water and dry by sqeezing in a tea cloth. Mix the potato with the onion, flour and eggs. Season with salt and pepper. Heat 2cm (¾in) of oil in a deep pan. Drop tablespoonfuls of the potato mixture into the hot oil, press each into a round, flat patty with the back of a spoon and fry until darkish brown and crisp on

both sides. As the latkes are fried, drain them on kitchen paper and lightly season again.
- To serve, divide the eel among the plates, trying to keep the pieces of fillet as big as possible. Beside them place 2 latkes and garnish with the rocket dressed in the walnut oil. Pass the relish separately.

Chef's tip

Use your butcher and fishmonger, rather than always buying meat and fish from the supermarket. If they won't bone out or fillet for you, try another shop.

Autumn

Fish Sausages with Sauce Vierge

The idea of sausages made of fish rather than pork is a strange idea, but they're a great way of using up the trimmings of delicately flavoured but expensive fish. And they have the great advantage of being able to be made in advance, then browned and reheated just before they're needed. The raw (vierge) tomato sauce/salsa is a perfect foil for the creamy richness of the sausages.

Serves 4
Preparation time: 1 hour
Cooking time: 40 minutes

325g (11½oz) white fish fillets (cod, whiting, monkfish), skinned and boned
50g (scant 2oz) fresh crab meat
4 scallops, with the corals, cut into 1cm (½in) pieces
1 egg white
150ml (5floz) double cream
pinch of cayenne pepper
1 tablespoon chopped fresh chervil
salt and pepper
Sauce Vierge (see page 230) to serve

For the pepper-lined timbales
2 red peppers
675g (1½lb) parsnips, peeled, quartered and cored
2 eggs
75g (2½oz) Parmesan, freshly grated
about 170ml (6floz) double cream

- Cut the white fish into small pieces and place in the container of a food processor. Add the crab meat and scallops. Chill for 30 minutes.
- Add the egg white and process until smooth. With the machine still running, pour in the cream, making sure that you complete this stage within 10 seconds (if over-processed, the mixture tends to curdle). Season with the cayenne, salt and pepper. Fold in the chervil.
- Divide the mixture into 8 portions and spoon on to 8 pieces of cling film, placing the mixture slightly to one side. Form the mixture into sausage shapes,

about 12cm (5in) long, then carefully roll up in the cling film, twisting the ends firmly to seal. Set aside in the fridge.
- To make the timbales, roast and peel the peppers (see Roasted Pepper and Aubergine Terrine, page 36). Divide each into 4 strips. Butter 4 dariole moulds or other small ovenproof moulds. Line with the pepper strips. Cook the parsnips in boiling salted water for about 15 minutes or until soft. Drain, then return to the empty hot pan to dry for 2 minutes. Put the parsnips into a blender or food processor and process with the eggs, cheese and enough cream to form a stiff paste. Spoon into the pepper-lined moulds. Set in a bain marie or roasting tin of water and simmer gently on top of the stove for 40 minutes or until a skewer inserted into the centre comes out clean and dry.
- To cook the sausages, fill a large, deep frying pan with water and bring to a gentle simmer. Reduce the heat and poach the sausages for 8 minutes.
- Transfer the sausages to a bowl of cold water and leave to cool for 2 minutes. Then lift the sausages out of the water and remove the cling film.
- Preheat the grill to medium.
- Brush each sausage with a little oil and grill for 8 minutes, turning occasionally, until golden on all sides. Serve hot with the sauce vierge and the timbales, turned out of their moulds.

Autumn

Steamed Cod with Ginger and Rice Wine

Steaming is a very gentle cooking method, perfect for delicate sweet fish. I can think of no improvement to this classically Chinese dish, which I first made on Ross's Foreign Assignment for ITN. The sesame oil is applied to the hot fish and gives off the most wonderful aroma, but be warned that a little goes a long way. A dry sherry could replace the rice wine.

Serves 2
Preparation time: 5 minutes
Cooking time: 10 minutes

a 2cm (¾in) piece of peeled fresh ginger, cut into matchsticks
2 spring onions, cut into 2cm (¾in) pieces
1 garlic clove, sliced
2 cod steaks, each about 170g (6oz)
60ml (2floz) rice wine
a few drops of toasted sesame oil
salt and white pepper

- Take a steamer and use a plate that will fit into it, but not too snugly because you want the steam to surround the fish. Arrange the ginger, spring onions and garlic on the plate and top with the fish steaks. Sprinkle with the rice wine and season with salt and a little pepper.
- Steam for 10 minutes, checking for doneness near the end. (Obviously, thicker pieces of fish take longer to cook.)
- Sprinkle a few drops of sesame oil over the fish and serve.

Winter

Hake in Serrano Ham with Capers and Saffron Pasta

Hake, a delicious, flaky white fish, is vastly underrated in this country, but is consumed in enormous amounts in the Iberian peninsula. In fact, most of the catch from this country goes there, to better prices than it would get on the quay. If you can't find hake, this method also works well with cod and haddock. The dish was inspired by a trip to the south of Spain, to cook paella for 200 on the beach at Torremolinos for GMTV. The flavours are pure southern Spain.

Serves 6
Preparation time: 25 minutes
Cooking time: 10 minutes

6 pieces of hake fillet, cut from the thick part, each about 150g (5½oz)
6 slices Serrano *or* Parma ham
4 tablespoons plain flour
6 tablespoons olive oil
6 sprigs of fresh chervil to garnish

For the pasta
300g (10½oz) dried tagliolini *or* similar thin noodles
juice of ½ lemon
pinch of saffron threads

150g (5½oz) chilled butter, cut into pieces

For the sauce
280g (10oz) shelled fresh peas or frozen petit pois
225g (8oz) frozen broad beans, thawed and skinned
2 tablespoons good capers, rinsed and drained
2 tablespoons chopped parsley
juice of ½ lemon

- The fish should be with its skin but scaled, as the skin is such a pretty silver and will show through the cooked ham. Wrap each piece in a slice of ham, then dredge with flour. Heat a little of the olive oil and add the fish, serving side down. Fry for 2–3 minutes or until browned and crispy, then turn and fry the other side until just cooked. Remove and keep warm in a low oven. Set the pan aside.

- Cook the pasta in boiling salted water until *al dente*.
- Meanwhile, for the sauce, blanch fresh peas in boiling water for 1 minute, then drain. Frozen petit pois only need to be thawed. Set aside.
- Heat the lemon juice in a saucepan with the same quantity of water and the saffron. Beat in the chilled butter. Keep warm to maintain the emulsion. When the pasta is cooked, drain well and dress in the butter sauce. Using a long-pronged carving fork, form skeins in much the same way as one eats spaghetti and pile on one side of individual plates or on to a large serving platter. Keep hot.
- Drain off most of the oil from the fish pan, then add the peas, beans, capers and parsley to the pan and gently warm through. (Too much heat will change the colour of the ingredients.) Add the rest of the oil and the lemon juice, season and mix well.
- Place each piece of fish on a pile of the vegetables next to the saffron pasta and use the warmed oil mixture as a sauce. Garnish with chervil and serve.

Winter

Potato Blinis, Gravadlax and Citrus Basil Dressing

The glutinous properties of the potato – which must never be blended in a food processor for mash – are called into action for these pancakes. The hot potato mixture absorbs the flour and egg proteins to make a very versatile batter. The blinis turn out very crisp, but need to be eaten quickly.

Serves 8
Preparation time: 2 hours plus 24 hours resting
Cooking time: 10 minutes

For the gravadlax
a 600g (1lb 5oz) piece of salmon fillet, as fresh as possible
handful of coarse salt
handful of sugar
12 juniper berries, crushed
4 tablespoons chopped fresh dill leaves

For the potato blinis
250g (9oz) potatoes
75ml (2½floz) hot milk
45g (1½oz) plain flour
2 egg yolks
2 tablespoons double cream
3 egg whites
70g (scant 2½oz) clarified butter

For the dressing
8 tablespoons olive oil
2 tablespoons fresh lime juice
2 sticks lemon grass, tender part only, finely chopped
15g (½oz) fresh basil leaves, shredded

To finish
125g (4½oz) crème fraîche
sprigs of fresh dill

- The gravadlax needs to be made 24 hours before serving. Take a non-corrosive dish or tray and lay the salmon in it, skin side down. Mix together the salt, sugar, juniper berries and dill and rub into the exposed flesh, piling the excess on top of the fish. Wrap closely in cling film and refrigerate for 24 hours. Half way through this time, turn the fish over on to the remaining salt/sugar mixture.

- Brush the salmon and then wipe off the excess salt/sugar mixture. Carve into very fine slices. Arrange on a plate, slightly overlapping, cover with cling film and keep in a cool place until ready to serve.
- For the blinis, cook the potatoes in their skins in boiling salted water, then drain and peel. Mash with the milk and leave to stand for 1 hour.
- In a food processor, purée the mashed potatoes with the flour. With the motor running, add the egg yolks, cream and then the whites. Season with salt and pepper.
- Make the dressing with the oil, lime juice and lemon grass. Set aside.
- Fry spoonfuls of the potato mixture, in batches, in the clarified butter until golden brown on both sides.
- Top each blini with a small blob of crème fraîche and lay gravadlax on to each to resemble a hat. Top with a sprig of dill. Add the basil to the citrus dressing, pour round the finished blinis and serve.

Chef's tip

To get the most juice from a lime, either roll it on the work surface or microwave for 10 seconds.

Winter

Sea Bass Roll with Beetroot Gnocchi

This is based on a dish I made from a most extraordinary bag on Ready, Steady Cook, *which included mackerel and beetroot. In fact, the two worked very well together. I have substituted sea bass for the mackerel in the version here because to many people mackerel is beyond the pale and sea bass is much more popular. Use either as you wish, or even herring.*

Serves 8
Preparation time: 1 hour
Cooking time: 40 minutes

1 large red onion
2 tomatoes, about 400g (14oz) total
1 aubergine, about 400g (14oz)
2 garlic cloves, chopped
4 tablespoons olive oil
2 sea bass, each about 1.25kg (2¾lb), filleted
salt and pepper

Fresh Tomato Sauce (see page 228) to serve

For the beetroot gnocchi
300g (10½oz) potatoes
300g (10½oz) beetroot
150g (5½oz) plain flour
olive oil to finish

- To make the gnocchi, cook the potatoes, in their skins, in boiling salted water until tender. (The reason the potatoes are not peeled before cooking is they absorb more water if peeled.) Drain. Peel when bearable to pick up, but the hotter the better.
- While the potatoes are cooking, cook and peel the beetroot. Purée in a food processor.
- Put the potatoes through a potato ricer or mash very thoroughly. Mix with the beetroot purée and season. Add the flour whilst the mixture is still hot to make a soft dough. (The more flour added, the more easily handled the mixture, but the more leaden the gnocchi will be.)

- Break off pieces and roll into sausages about 2cm (¾in) thick. Cut across into 1cm (½in) lengths and pinch each slightly. Cover and set aside.
- Preheat the oven to 200°C/400°F/Gas 6.
- Chop the onion, tomatoes and aubergine into 3mm (⅛in) dice. Fry with the garlic in the oil until softened. Season well. Set aside.
- Remove any remaining bones from the sea bass fillets. Place one fillet, skin side down, on a large piece of oiled foil. Cover with half of the vegetable mixture. Set another fillet on top, placing it top to tail and skin side out. Roll in the foil and secure the ends. You should have a sausage of the same thickness all the way down. Repeat with the remaining sea bass fillets and vegetable mixture
- Roast in the oven for 35 minutes, then remove and leave to rest for 5 minutes
- Meanwhile, add the gnocchi to a pan of boiling salted water and poach until they float to the surface, at which point they are ready. Drain well and dress with olive oil.
- Cut the sea bass rolls into 4cm (1½in) slices and then peel off the foil. Serve with the beetroot gnocchi and tomato sauce or with salad and vinaigrette.

Winter

Smoked Cod's Roe with Pak Choi and Black Beans

I've always really liked salty things and cod's roe is no exception. As part of an antipasti plate it is a great asset, with its spreadability and fabulous richness. If you prefer, you can use lentils instead of black beans in this recipe.

Serves 4
Preparation time: 40 minutes plus overnight soaking
Cooking time: 1–1¼ hours

150g (5½oz) dried black beans, soaked overnight
200ml (7floz) olive oil
scant 3 tablespoons lemon juice
2 tablespoons chopped fresh coriander
1 teaspoon finely chopped fresh red chilli
4 small pak choi, quartered lenthways
500g (1lb 2oz) smoked cod's roe
salt and pepper

- Cook the beans in unsalted water until soft. Drain, rinse and refresh.
- To make the dressing, mix the oil and lemon juice together and season with salt and pepper.
- Mix the beans with the coriander and chilli and dress with half the dressing. Set aside.
- Add the pak choi to the remaining dressing and allow to marinate for about 20 minutes or until the pieces start to wilt.
- To serve, drain the pak choi and pile on to each plate. Add a slice of cod's roe and then the bean salad. Alternatively, the flesh from the cod's roe can be whisked up with the dressing drained from the pak choi. Serve with plenty of crusty bread.

Winter

Mackerel and Chick Pea Stew

The south of Spain has a cuisine with a very rich history. The visiting Moors left their culinary influencess; the Arabs contributed saffron and chick peas.

Serves 6
Preparation time: 40 minutes
Cooking time: 30 minutes

6 small mackerel, cleaned and heads removed
plain flour
4 tablespoons olive oil
1kg (2¼lb) fresh tomatoes, peeled and finely chopped or puréed
500ml (17floz) fish stock
pinch of saffron threads
a 400g (14oz) can chick peas, drained

For the picada
6 garlic cloves
1 red pepper, roasted and peeled (see Roasted Pepper and Aubergine Terrine, page 36) then chopped
12 blanched almonds
12 hazelnuts, skinned
1 slice white bread, fried in oil until golden brown
3 tablespoons finely chopped parsley
a few drops of white wine
a few drops of olive oil
salt and pepper

- Dredge the mackerel in a little flour, then fry in the hot olive oil until browned on both sides. Remove with a slotted spoon and reserve.
- Put the *picada* ingredients, except the oil, in a food processor or blender and process until almost completely smooth. Work in the oil, then fry in the fish pan for 1 minute, stirring.
- Add the tomatoes and fish stock to the *picada* and cook for 5 minutes or until thickened, stirring occasionally.
- Return the fish to the pan together with the saffron and chick peas. Simmer for 15 minutes. Test the fish for doneness and season with salt and pepper, serve.

POULTRY
& FEATHERED GAME

SPRING

Chicken and Tamarind Salad

When I filmed a series on Thai food for Carlton Food Network this was the most popular dish among the crew. Tamarind, which is the principal ingredient in HP sauce, has a sweet-sour flavour and depth of taste that is quite extraordinary. This dish is great made with left-over chicken or turkey, and can be prepared well in advance.

Serves 4
Preparation time: 30 minutes
Cooking time: 20 minutes

2 large chicken breasts
3 tablespoons tamarind water (see page 231)
2 tablespoons fish sauce
1 tablespoon sugar
1 tablespoon lime juice
a 5cm (2in) piece of lemon grass, thinly sliced into rings
2 tablespoons fresh ginger cut into fine matchsticks
6 small shallots, sliced into thin ovals
3 fresh lime leaves, thinly sliced
1 tablespoon chopped fresh coriander
1 tablespoon green peppercorns packed in brine, drained
1 large fresh red chilli, sliced into oval rings
1 leek, very finely shredded
oil for deep-frying

To finish
crisp lettuce leaves
fresh coriander leaves

- Preheat the grill.
- Grill the chicken breasts until golden brown and cooked through. With your fingers, tear the meat into small shreds and set aside to cool.
- In a small saucepan, heat the tamarind water with the fish sauce and sugar, stirring until the sugar dissolves. Remove from the heat and add the lime juice. Stir in the shredded chicken, mixing well. Add the lemon grass, ginger, shallots, lime leaves, coriander and peppercorns and stir well. Add the chilli and stir.
- Arrange the lettuce leaves around a platter and place the chicken mixture in the centre.
- Deep-fry the shreds of leek until they look like straw. Drain on kitchen paper.
- Garnish the chicken salad with coriander leaves and the leeks. Serve warm.

POULTRY & FEATHERED GAME

Spring

Smoked Quail and Asparagus Salad with Polenta Chips

Quail have been farm-raised for over 2000 years and are very tasty, especially smoked like this. Any good deli or butcher will get smoked quail in for you if they are not in stock, but try not to use frozen ones, as they can be rather dry. The crisp asparagus and orange vinaigrette cut through the richness of the quail meat. Polenta is a vastly over-rated ingredient, usually more like wallpaper paste, but when deep-fried the texture is greatly improved. Sausages of ready-made polenta are now sold in supermarkets, which takes all the drudgery out of stirring the wretched stuff for 40 or so minutes. Halved new potatoes, fried cut side down until really crisp, would suffice as an accompaniment.

Serves 6
Preparation time: 40 minutes
Cooking time: 10 minutes

12 smoked quail
500g (1lb 2oz) thick asparagus
3 oranges (blood oranges would be impressive)
500g (1lb 2oz) ready-made polenta, cut into 4 x 1cm (1½ x ½in) sticks
oil for deep-frying

2 heads frisée, separated into leaves

For the dressing
125ml (4½floz) olive oil
1 teaspoon caster sugar
1 teaspoon Dijon mustard
salt and black pepper

- Carve the quail into neat pieces and reserve.
- Trim and peel the asparagus, then blanch in boiling salted water for 90 seconds. (Peeling is not entirely necessary, but it does improve the appearance and can help if the asparagus is a little woody at the end of the season.) Drain and refresh.

Poultry & Feathered Game

- Zest the oranges with a citrus zester, or use a potato peeler and then slice into very fine shreds. Peel the oranges of all the white pith and cut into segments, reserving any released juice.
- To make the dressing, whisk the ingredients with the reserved orange juice and season with salt and plenty of fresh black pepper. If there is a lot of orange juice and the dressing won't emulsify, add a little more mustard.
- Deep-fry the polenta sticks in oil heated to 190°C/375°F or until a day-old cube of bread browns in 1 minute, until crispy and golden brown. Drain well on kitchen paper and season.
- Toss the frisée with the dressing, the shreds of orange zest and the asparagus. Pile on to 6 plates. Arrange the quail and the polenta chips on and around the piles and serve immediately. Alternatively, this would make a splendid buffet dish on a large platter. Just watch your guests ferreting about for another piece of quail!

Wine note

With the smoky richness of the quail and the crisp acidity of the asparagus, try a really good-quality Riesling from Germany which will marry well with both. At 10 years or older, this sometimes underrated grape takes on wonderful deep, rich flavours.

SPRING

BONED CHICKEN WITH APRICOTS AND PECANS

This dish is perfect for entertaining, being economical and able to be prepared in advance – a cold main course can really help the stress levels! The recipe here was heavily influenced by one of Alastair Little's, which I used while teaching for his company in Tuscany. A boned chicken provides a perfect wrapping for many types of fillings. A forcemeat of nuts and herbs makes a heavier but delicious replacement for chicken breasts.

Serves 8
Preparation time: 30 minutes plus overnight chilling
Cooking time: 1½ hours

a 1.35 kg (3lb) free-range chicken, boned (ask your butcher to do this)
100g (3½oz) pecan halves
100g (3½oz) plump dried apricots
2 large chicken breasts
4 thin slices Parma ham
1 glass dry white wine
1 tablespoon olive oil
fresh coriander and flat-leaf parsley leaves to garnish
lemon wedges to serve

For the parsley pesto
50g (scant 2oz) fresh parsley
2 garlic cloves, peeled
2 tablespoons pine nuts, toasted
4 tablespoons extra virgin olive oil
3 tablespoons freshly grated Parmesan
salt and pepper

- Preheat the oven to 200°C/400°F/Gas 6.
- To make the pesto, process all the ingredients except the cheese in a small blender until smooth. Stir in the Parmesan.
- Flatten the boned chicken on the work surface, skin side down, and spread half the pesto over the bird. Layer the pecans and apricots on top. Wrap each chicken breast in 2 slices of Parma ham and place these centrally on the bird. Spread the remaining pesto on top of them. Wrap the boned bird around the

filling ingredients to make a neat joint. Put the joint in a terrine or 900g (2lb) loaf tin.
- Pour the wine around the joint. Brush it with the olive oil and season with salt and pepper. Cover loosely with foil. Roast for 1½ hours, removing the foil and basting after 1 hour. Baste again 20 minutes later.
- Remove from the oven and leave to cool in the tin, then refrigerate overnight.
- Remove from the tin, place on a board and cut across into slices about 2.5cm (1in) thick. Drizzle a little extra virgin olive oil over the slices and scatter fresh coriander and flat-leaf parsley round the slices on each plate. Serve with wedges of lemon.

Wine note

With the creamy white flesh of the chicken and the sweet fruitiness of the apricots, a New Zealand or Chilean Chardonnay would be perfect.

SPRING

SUPREME OF CHICKEN WITH AUBERGINE FRITTERS AND BEAN SALAD

I developed this recipe for a 5-day cruise I did on the QE2 to New York. I went with GMTV and was privileged to spend the evenings dancing 'til dawn with Liz Earle and Lorraine Kelly. If ever there was a way to work off fried aubergines, that was it. Being greeted by the Statue of Liberty at 5am, having danced all night, is an experience I'll never forget.

Serves 4
Preparation time: 40 minutes
Cooking time: 25 minutes

4 chicken supremes
200g (7oz) frozen chopped spinach, thawed and squeezed dry
150g (5½oz) ricotta cheese
freshly grated nutmeg
4 slices Parma ham
8 large fresh sage leaves, without stalks
15g (½oz) fresh basil leaves
100ml (3½floz) extra virgin olive oil
150g (5½oz) French beans, blanched and refreshed
150g (5½oz) canned butter beans, drained and rinsed
150g (5½oz) canned chick peas, drained and rinsed
100ml (3½floz) Basic Vinaigrette (see page 229)
salt and pepper

For the aubergine fritters
4 large slices aubergine, cut 1cm (½in) thick
150g (5½oz) fresh breadcrumbs
15g (½oz) fresh sage leaves, thinly sliced
100g (3½oz) Parmesan, freshly grated
70g (scant 2½oz) plain flour
2 eggs, lightly beaten
150ml (5floz) olive oil

- Preheat the oven to 200°C/400°F/Gas 6.
- For the fritters, sprinkle the aubergine slices with salt, then leave to drain for 30 minutes; rinse and pat dry.
- Meanwhile, with a long, sharp knife, cut a pocket in each of the supremes from one end to the other.
- Mix the spinach with the ricotta and season to taste with nutmeg, salt and pepper. Stuff the pockets in the supremes with the spinach mixture. Wrap each in a slice of Parma ham, including 2 sage leaves between the chicken and ham.
- Wrap each supreme in a double thickness of oiled foil and twist the ends to secure. Roast for 25 minutes. When the chicken has finished cooking, remove from the oven and leave to rest for 5 minutes.
- While the chicken is roasting, make the fritters. Mix together the breadcrumbs, sage and Parmesan on a plate. Dip the aubergine slices first in the flour to coat all over, then in the eggs and, finally, in the crumb mixture, patting it on gently. Fry in the olive oil on a moderate heat until well browned on both sides. Drain on kitchen paper and keep warm.
- Blend the basil with the extra virgin oil. Dress the mixed beans and chick peas with the vinaigrette.
- On each of 4 plates, mound one-quarter of the bean salad. Slice the supremes and arrange round the salad. Lean a fritter against each mound and drizzle the basil oil around the edge of the plates.

Wine note

With this very savoury dish I would serve a light Italian red such as Valpolicella made by the excellent firm of Tedeschi.

Spring

Guinea Fowl Supreme on an Artichoke Cake

Guinea fowl looks entirely different from a chicken in the feather, but surprisingly similar in a butcher's shop. The flavour is much better than ordinary chicken, although a free-range chicken could be substituted in this dish. Supremes are just the breasts with the first wing bone still attached, for that restaurant-quality presentation. Supermarkets now sell these in packs of two. This is a great way to use up left-over risotto – it's almost nicer the second day, with the creamy interior hiding underneath the crisp surface.

Serves 6
Preparation time: 1 hour
Cooking time: 25 minutes

2 tablespoons olive oil
6 guinea fowl supremes
1 medium onion, finely chopped
2 tablespoons brandy
250ml (8½floz) good chicken stock
1 beef tomato *or* 2 plum tomatoes, peeled, seeded and finely diced
6 large sprigs of fresh chervil or flat-leaf parsley

For the artichoke cakes
a 425g (15oz) can artichoke hearts, drained
½ quantity of plain risotto (see Porcini Risotto, page 48, made without the porcini)
50g (scant 2oz) plain flour
3 eggs, beaten
200g (7oz) fresh breadcrumbs
4 tablespoons olive oil

- Preheat the oven to 200°C/400°F/Gas 6.
- Heat the oil in a frying pan and brown the supremes, skin side down first, for 3 minutes on each side. Transfer to a roasting tin and place in the oven to roast for 10–12 minutes or until done (test with the tip of a knife: the juice that runs out of the meat should be clear).
- While the supremes are cooking, fry the onion in the oil remaining in the frying pan to colour slightly. Deglaze with the brandy, which will flame as the alcohol

burns off, then pour in the chicken stock and boil to reduce to a syrupy consistency. Set this sauce aside.
- To make the artichoke cakes, drain the artichokes very well as the brine they come in is unpleasant. (I use a salad spinner to get it all out, but squashing in a tea towel also does the trick.) Finely chop the artichokes and fold through the risotto. Form into 6 round cakes about 6cm (2½in) in diameter and 3cm (1¼in) thick. (Don't make them too thick or the heat will not penetrate to the centre when they're fried.) Flour, egg and crumb the cakes, then gently fry in the olive oil until they are a good rich brown on both sides. Keep warm until the supremes are ready.
- To serve, place an artichoke cake on each warmed plate and top with a supreme. Strain the sauce (reheated if necessary) and mix in the raw tomato and any juices released from the supremes, then spoon round the cakes. Garnish with the chervil.

SUMMER

CHICKEN AND MOZZARELLA ROLLS WITH SAFFRON MAYO

Saffron is the most evocative of spices. Britain once grew enormous amounts, in Saffron Walden, and exported it to Turkey. Now the best comes from La Mancha in Spain. The colour of this dish is wonderful and it really is worthwhile trying. You will have more saffron mayo than you need here, but the remainder can be enjoyed in salads or sandwiches.

Serves 4
Preparation time: 45 minutes
Cooking time: 25 minutes

4 chicken supremes
140g (5oz) buffalo mozzarella, finely diced
150g (5½oz) fresh white breadcrumbs
2 garlic cloves, crushed
1 beef tomato, peeled, seeded and finely diced
4 slices Parma ham
15g (½oz) fresh basil leaves
salt and pepper

For the saffron mayo
2 egg yolks
2 teaspoons Dijon mustard
2 teaspoons caster sugar
pinch of saffron threads
2 teaspoons white wine vinegar
250ml (8½floz) sunflower oil

For the charred asparagus
1kg (2¼lb) fresh asparagus, trimmed
100ml (3½floz) extra virgin olive oil
50g (scant 2oz) Parmesan, flaked

- To make the saffron mayo, whisk together all the ingredients except the oil until amalgamated. Add the oil in a slow, steady stream, whisking to combine. Store in the refrigerator, covered with cling film pressed on to the surface of the mayonnaise so that oxidization doesn't occur.
- Preheat the oven to 200°C/400°F/Gas 6.
- With a long, sharp knife, cut a pocket in each of the supremes. Set aside.

- Mix together the mozzarella, breadcrumbs, garlic and tomato and season with salt and pepper. Stuff the pockets in the supremes with the mozzarella mixture. Wrap each in a slice of Parma ham, including a few basil leaves between the chicken and ham.
- Wrap each supreme in a double thickness of oiled foil and twist the ends to secure. Roast for 25 minutes. When the chicken has finished cooking, remove from the oven and leave to rest for 5 minutes.
- While the chicken is roasting, prepare the asparagus. Blanch it in well-salted boiling water for 1–2 minutes, then drain and refresh. Char on a hot cast-iron grill pan for 2 minutes on each side. Serve warm drizzled with the oil and sprinkled with the Parmesan.
- Unwrap the supremes and cut each into 3 slices. Dress with the juices from the parcels and add a dollop of the saffron mayo to each plate. Serve with the charred asparagus and crusty bread.

Summer Jambalaya

A favourite in the American South, Cajun Jambalaya can be a simple dish of leftovers or elevated to gastronomic heights by using partridge and lobster. It is thought that the name comes from the French and African traditions of that part of the US: jambon (ham) à la (with) ya (African for rice). The trilogy of celery, green peppers and spring onions features heavily in Cajun cuisine.

Serves 8
Preparation time: 30 minutes
Cooking time: 50 minutes

60ml (2floz) sunflower oil
500g (1lb 2oz) cooking chorizo, cut into 5mm (¼in) rounds, *or* cooked ham in 1cm (½in) cubes
2 large onions, finely diced
1 bunch celery, stringed and diced, including the leaves
1 bunch spring onions, finely sliced
2 garlic cloves, finely chopped
1 fresh green chilli, seeded and finely chopped (optional)
300g (10½oz) basmati rice, washed
600ml (1 pint) tomato passata
1.2 litres (2 pints) chicken stock
3 fresh bay leaves *or* 2 dried bay leaves
3 sprigs of fresh thyme *or* 1 teaspoon dried thyme
3 tablespoons chopped fresh parsley
500g (1lb 2oz) cooked chicken meat, chopped
½ teaspoon ground cumin

- Heat the oil in a large pan and fry the chorizo or ham with the onions, celery, spring onions and garlic until the vegetables are soft but not coloured, about 10 minutes on a low heat. (The fat that runs out of the chorizo is bright red and carries the fat-soluble pigments from the paprika that it contains. This adds to the colour of the dish, but don't get it on your clothes as it really stains.)
- Add the rest of the ingredients and bring to the boil. Turn down the heat to very low and cover with a close-fitting lid. Simmer for 30 minutes, stirring once or twice. The dish shouldn't boil dry, but check near the end of the cooking time.
- Test the rice for doneness and serve.

SUMMER

Roast Duck with Prune and Apple Stuffing

Roast duck is one of my favourite things. As it cooks for quite a long time, it makes the whole house smell, which to my mind is very much a positive thing. The other upside to roasting duck is that it releases a great deal of fat, which is great for roasting potatoes or for making savoury pastry or the base for confit of duck (see the mallard recipe on page 115). Kept in the fridge, the fat lasts for ages. People often think of duck as being greasy, but following this method you should have no trouble producing perfect, crispy duck every time. The carcass, once carved and picked over, makes splendid stock for risottos and sauces.

Serves 4
Preparation time: 30 minutes
Cooking time: 1 hour 40 minutes

2 Barbary ducks, without giblets
1 large onion, finely chopped
30g (1oz) butter *or* duck fat from the last roast
1 cooking apple, peeled and finely chopped
2 eggs
150g (5½oz) prunes, stoned and roughly chopped
250g (9oz) fresh white breadcrumbs
1 teaspoon fresh thyme leaves *or* ½ teaspoon dried thyme
1 tablespoon plain flour
240ml (8floz) duck *or* chicken stock *or* water
salt and pepper
watercress to garnish

- Wash the ducks well and pierce the skin all over with a carving fork (take care not to pierce the flesh as that tends to dry it out). Place the ducks in a sink and pour two kettles of boiling water over them. Allow to cool.
- Preheat the oven to 160°C/325°F/Gas 3.
- Fry the onion in the butter or the duck fat to soften but not colour. Add the apple and fry briefly with the onion.

- Beat the eggs lightly with a little salt and pepper and stir into the prunes. Tip in the apple and onion mixture, add the breadcrumbs and thyme and mix well together. Pack this stuffing into the front cavity of the ducks (alternatively, it can be cooked separately in a foil-lined loaf tin).
- Place the ducks on a rack in a roasting tin and season with salt and pepper. Pour a little water into the roasting tin, to keep the roasting juices liquid. Roast for about 1 hour 40 minutes. When you start to smell duck, it's on its way to being done and when it looks gorgeous and the meat is coming away from the drumstick bone, it has probably finished cooking. Roast duck, like roast leg of lamb, should be very well cooked.
- Remove the ducks to a plate, cover with foil and a cloth and leave to rest. Drain off all but 1 tablespoon of fat from the roasting tin, then set it over a moderate heat. Add the flour and cook, stirring, for 1–2 minutes. Gradually stir in the stock or water and simmer to make a gravy. Season.
- Carve the birds and serve with the stuffing and gravy, garnished with watercress, and with vegetables of your choice.

Wine note

As this is a bit of a special dish, I would drink something a little better than an everyday wine. A 5-year-old red Burgundy from a village level, such as a Morey St Denis, would be perfect. And if you make this dish and are serving a decent drop, can I come?

Summer

Coronation Chicken with Shredded Chicory

Now a standby of summer cuisine in these sceptered isles, I can think of no finer dish to celebrate a coronation. The bitterness of the chicory works perfectly with the sweet chicken. A word on chutney: use a proper one, not jam masquerading as chutney, which has no flavour or bits of fruit or spices. Geeta's makes a spendid version full of chunks of mango, cloves and peppercorns.

Serves 6
Preparation time: 10 minutes
Cooking time: 30 minutes

6 skinless boneless chicken breasts
1–2 bay leaves
6 black peppercorns
6 tablespoons mango chutney
250g (9oz) Greek yogurt
30g (1oz) fresh coriander, finely chopped
¼ teaspoon ground cumin
¼ teaspoon chilli powder
¼ teaspoon ground cinnamon
3 ripe mangoes, peeled and cut into 1cm (½in) dice
3 heads white chicory, separated into leaves then shredded

- Place the chicken breasts in a pan with the bay leaves and peppercorns and cover with water, plus any left-over white wine you may have. Bring to a simmer and poach for 10 minutes. Check for doneness, then allow to cool in the poaching liquid (this encourages moistness).
- When the breasts are cold, drain and pat dry. Cut into 2cm (¾in) chunks.
- Mix together all the remaining ingredients except the chicory. Add the chicken and fold through.
- Spoon the chicken mixture on to a platter and pile the shredded chicory on top. Or, surround the chicken mixture, formed into a dome, with the whole chicory leaves sticking out, to resemble a crown.

SUMMER

GUINEA FOWL WITH LIME AND MONEYBAGS

This is a French/Asian dish in that it uses classical French technique and is inspired by Asian ingredients and traditions. Dim sum shaped like moneybags are eaten at New Year to encourage prosperity, and the garnish for this dish mirrors those.

Serves 6
Preparation time: 1 hour
Cooking time: 55 minutes

3 guinea fowl, each about 1kg (2¼lb)
3 whole limes
3 sprigs of fresh thyme
2 onions, roughly chopped
3 tablespoons Calvados
250ml (8½floz) chicken stock
50g (scant 2oz) butter
juice of another 3 limes
salt and pepper

For the moneybags
1 large onion, very thinly sliced

15g (½oz) butter
2 tablespoons caster sugar
2 tablespoons red wine vinegar
1 sheet filo pastry
6 fresh chives *or* 6 pieces spring onion green, blanched

To garnish
18 spring onions, trimmed
2 tablespoons stock
15g (½oz) butter

- Preheat the oven to 200°C/400°F/Gas 6.
- First make the moneybags. Fry the onion very gently in the butter until it starts to take on a good dark brown (not burnt) colour. Add the sugar and vinegar and continue to cook until you have a dry mass of sweetly scented onion marmalade. Allow to cool.
- Cut the sheet of filo into 6 squares. Pile a little of the marmalade on to each and gather up into a moneybag shape. Tie with a chive or blanched spring onion

green. Place on a buttered baking tray and bake for about 10 minutes or until golden brown. Keep warm. Turn the oven up to 220°C/425°F/Gas 7.
- Cut the wingtips off the guinea fowl. Bend the ankles back until the joint is dislocated then cut off. (By having clean joints, the flesh will contract over the cooking period and you will have neater pieces when the birds are carved.) Pierce the 3 whole limes with a fork and put one inside each guinea fowl together with a sprig of thyme and a little seasoning.
- Place the birds on a bed of chopped onions in a roasting tin (the onions will caramelize and give colour and flavour to the sauce). Roast for 40 minutes or until a skewer inserted into the thickest part of the thighs lets only clear juices out. Remove the guinea fowl to a warm platter, cover with foil and allow to rest for 10 minutes.
- Pour off any excess fat from the roasting tin, then deglaze with the Calvados. When the flames subside, add the stock and boil to reduce by half, scraping up any residues as you go. Strain into a saucepan, pressing well on the onions so they release all their juices.
- Whilst the sauce is boiling, blanch the spring onions in boiling salted water for 2 minutes; drain and refresh. Tie each once so you have 18 pretty garnishes.
- Carve each of the birds into thighs, legs and breast joints (keep the carcasses for well-flavoured additions to your stockpot). Add any released juices to the sauce and continue to boil. Return the carved joints to the oven for 5 minutes to reheat.
- Whisk the butter into the sauce to give it a gloss, and sharpen with the lime juice. Warm the spring onion knots in the stock and butter.
- Arrange the guinea fowl joints on individual plates. Garnish with the spring onion knots and the moneybags and pour the lime sauce around. Serve immediately, with roast potatoes and steamed green vegetables. Candied lime zest or fresh coriander could be used as extra garnishes.

Autumn

Roast Mallard, Cooked Two Ways

This is a delicious recipe, with the breasts and legs of the mallard treated entirely differently to achieve the best from both, and to introduce a variety of textures and flavours. Confit of duck is rightly continuing to be a fashionable dish around Britain. Its melting richness contrasts well with the rare breast meat. The trimmings are entirely optional, but few people need much excuse to make bread sauce (see page 229)! As with all roasted game birds, the gravy should be runny. Game chips are perfect accompaniments.

Serves 8
Preparation time: 20 minutes plus 24 hours marinating
Cooking time: 1 hour

4 mallard ducks
coarse salt (optional)
1kg (2¼lb) duck fat
32 shallots, peeled
3 tablespoons olive oil
1 onion, finely chopped
3 tablespoons brandy
3 tablespoons port
125ml (4½floz) red wine
1 tablespoon tomato purée
12 juniper berries
250ml (8½floz) chicken stock
salt and pepper
8 small bunches of watercress to garnish

- Have your butcher remove the legs from the ducks and then trim them, to form 4 breast joints, with the undercarriage cut away. (This is of no real use for stock as wild ducks will tend to impart a bitter flavour.)
- If you have time, rub the legs with coarse salt and pepper and leave in a cool place for 24 hours. This seasons, strengthens and dehydrates the flesh, but in this case, as the legs are so small, it is not an essential step.
- Preheat the oven to 150°C/300°F/Gas 2.

- If you have salted the legs, rinse and dry them. Place them in a roasting tin with the duck fat and poach in the oven for about 1 hour or until very tender – a small knife should go through without any resistance. Drain the confits and set aside. Turn the oven up to 200°C/400°F/Gas 6.
- Roll the shallots in 1 tablespoon olive oil and season. Roast for 12 minutes, shaking the tin twice so they colour evenly. Remove and keep warm. Turn the oven up to 225°C/425°F/Gas 7.
- Score the skin of the breast joints slightly to allow the fat to run. Heat the remaining olive oil in a frying pan and brown the joints all over. Transfer to a roasting tin and roast for 12 minutes for rare. When the breast joints are cooked, leave to rest for 5 minutes.
- While the breast joints are roasting, add the onion to the frying pan and cook until browned. Deglaze with the brandy, then add the port and reduce by half. Add the wine, tomato purée, juniper berries and stock and reduce until a gravy is formed. Strain into a saucepan and set aside.
- Crisp the duck leg confits under a preheated grill for 5 minutes.
- Slice the breasts from the bone; pour all the released juices into the gravy.
- Serve each person a breast sliced into three and a leg. Garnish with the roasted shallots and watercress. Either flood the plate with the gravy or serve it separately.

Autumn

Cassoulet

Like all classic dishes, cassoulet has many imitators – one being the pork and baked beans so loved by American cowboys. All versions of the dish are centred round white beans and a mixture of meats to give a balance of flavours and textures. The cassoulet here is unashamedly rich, very much an 'LBL' (long, boozy lunch) dish. The only side order with this is sleep! I once enjoyed a superb cassoulet and LBL with Bill Knott when he wrote for the excellent but now sadly extinct Eat Soup.

Serves 8
Preparation time: 1 hour plus overnight chilling and soaking
Cooking time: about 10 hours

2 ducks
1 tablespoon black peppercorns
1 tablespoon coriander seeds
handful of coarse salt
4 large onions
1 bunch celery
bunch of parsley stalks
1 bulb garlic, separated into cloves
450g (1lb) dried haricot beans
a 450g (1lb) piece of green bacon
12 cloves
450g (1lb) tomatoes, peeled and pulped
bunch of fresh thyme
450g (1lb) neck of lamb, trimmed of silverskin and excess fat
450g (1lb) best coarse-textured pork sausages
5 slices white toast bread, made into crumbs

- Start the preparation the day before. Preheat the oven to 200°C/400°F/Gas 6.
- Joint the ducks into legs and breasts; set the carcasses and fat aside. Trim the breasts and reserve for another recipe (or freeze). Wash and dry the legs. Toss the peppercorns, coriander seeds and coarse salt together and rub into the legs. Place in a non-corrosive container and refrigerate, covered, for 24 hours.
- Roast the duck carcasses and 2 of the onions, quartered, for 1 hour. In another roasting tin in the same oven, render the duck fat and skin, pouring off the liquid fat into a bowl at 15-minute intervals. Continue until all the fat has been rendered (treat this with respect and reverence). Discard the skin and allow the fat to cool.

- Transfer the roasted duck carcasses to a large pot and add all the celery except the outer 2 sticks. Cover with cold water and add the parsley stalks and all but 3 large cloves of the garlic. Bring to the boil. Skim, then reduce the heat to a simmer. Continue simmering and skimming for 3 hours. Strain the stock and reserve. (This makes far too much, but is delicious and can be used in many other dishes.)
- Put the beans to soak in plenty of cold water overnight, and then retire.
- The next day, take the fat and rind from the bacon in one piece. Drain the beans and put into a large vessel with the bacon fat and rind. Add the reserved sticks of celery and 1 peeled onion stuck with the cloves. Cover with cold water and bring to the boil. Simmer for about 1 hour or until the beans are tender but not mushy. (Do not add salt during the cooking or the beans will not soften.) Drain the beans and reserve; discard the onion and celery. Pare all the fat from bacon rind, then set the rind aside.
- Preheat the oven to 180°C/350°F/Gas 4.
- Rinse the salt and spices from the duck legs and pat dry. Coat the bottom of an ovenproof dish or baking tray with some of the rendered duck fat. Lay the legs, skin side up, in the dish and pour over the remaining duck fat (a snug tray is best for this). Poach in the oven for about 2 hours or until a sharp knife will easily pierce the meat. (If not using straight away, pour the fat into a bowl and put the duck legs in another bowl, sealing with some of the fat; keep both in the fridge until you can resist no longer.)
- Finely chop the remaining onion and fry in a little of the duck fat until softened. Add the reserved cloves of garlic, finely chopped, and the tomatoes. Pour in 475ml (16floz) of the stock. Boil until reduced by half.
- Chop the reserved pork rind into tiny squares and mix with the beans and tomato 'sauce' in a large bowl. Add the thyme leaves and stir (thyme leaves are most easily removed by freezing the washed and dried bunch and then rubbing the stalks together).
- Chop the bacon and the neck of lamb into 2.5cm (1in) pieces, and brown quickly in a little duck fat. Drain and reserve. Skin the duck legs confit and chop or shred the flesh into similar-sized pieces. Grill the sausages and chop into similar-sized pieces.
- When ready to cook the cassoulet, preheat the oven to 160°C/325°F/Gas 3.

- Spoon half of the bean mixture into a large casserole of about 6 litres (10½ pints) capacity. Layer the meats on the beans and cover with the rest of the beans. Sprinkle one-third of the breadcrumbs over the beans. Bake for 1 hour.
- Stir the now toasted crumbs into the bean mixture and re-cover with another third of the crumbs. Repeat after another hour. After 3 hours the dish is ready to serve. If on stirring, the dish looks particularly dry, add a little stock. The finished dish should be dryish and not too runny.
- Serve with a salad dressed with salt and walnut oil.

Wine note

A really delicious and robust red would suit this dish well. The red Bandol wines of Provence are perfect for this, as are the Californian versions labelled under the grape variety Mourvèdre.

Autumn

Pheasant Braised in Cider

Pheasant is often plentiful and cheap near the end of the season. Then it benefits from more gentle cooking than just the simple roasting that is more appropriate earlier on. I have spent many weekends with friends in Shropshire, surely the most beautiful of English counties, where fresh pheasant and Herefordshire cider featured heavily. I used to stay in a gorgeous castle, an outlier of Ludlow Castle, where I could pick herbs from the kitchen garden and then cook dishes such as this for house parties of up to two dozen.

Serves 6
Preparation time: 50 minutes
Cooking time: 1 hour

1 brace of pheasants
2 tablespoons olive oil
250g (9oz) streaky bacon, cut into lardons
24 small button onions, peeled
bunch of fresh thyme
3 garlic cloves, finely chopped
600ml (1 pint) good well-flavoured cider
pepper

To thicken the sauce (optional)
25g (scant 1oz) butter
2 tablespoons plain flour

- Cut each of the pheasants into 8 joints and brown in the oil in a frying pan. Remove to a flameproof casserole.
- Brown the bacon lardons and onions in the fat remaining in the pan, then sprinkle around the pheasant pieces. Push the thyme and garlic in and season with plenty of pepper.
- Tip the fat from the frying pan and deglaze with a splash of the cider, stirring to mix in all the residues from the bottom of the pan. Pour over the pheasant pieces and add the rest of the cider.
- Bring to the boil, then reduce to a simmer. Cover and cook on a low simmer for 1 hour. Check for doneness. If the casserole dries out, just add a little stock to moisten it.
- If you like, the sauce can be thickened with the butter and flour worked into a paste; stir into the sauce and bring back to the boil.
- Serve with loads of mash.

Autumn

Chicken Legs stuffed with Chestnuts and Black Pudding

Although a cheap dish, this has all the gutsy earthiness that good peasant food can offer. The recipe was inspired by a shoot I did in southern Spain, in Gaucìn near Ronda, where local ingredients seemed to fly at each other and suggest dishes to me.

Serves 8
Preparation time: 1 hour
Cooking time: 50 minutes

8 large chicken legs, each about 300g (10½oz)
100g (3½oz) onion, finely diced
1 tablespoon olive oil
1 garlic clove, finely chopped
1 egg
200g (7oz) vacuum-packed chestnuts, very finely diced
200g (7oz) black pudding, very finely diced
2 teaspoons fresh thyme leaves *or* 1 teaspoon dried thyme
24 slices Speck *or* 16 slices Parma ham
salt and pepper

- Preheat the oven to 200°C/400°F/Gas 6.
- Remove the thigh bone from the chicken legs (or have your butcher do this for you).
- Fry the onion in the oil until translucent but not coloured. Add the garlic and fry for a further 30 seconds. Remove from the heat. Beat the egg in a large bowl with a pinch of salt and generous grindings of black pepper. Add the chestnuts, black pudding and onion and mix well. Add the thyme leaves and give another grinding of black pepper. Set this stuffing aside.
- For each chicken leg, lay 3 slices of Speck, or 2 slices of Parma ham, slightly overlapping, on the work surface. Place the legs, skin side down, on the ham so

all the flesh will be covered but the leg bone is exposed. Divide the stuffing into 8 portions, and use to fill the cavity in the chicken legs left by removing the thigh bone. Wrap the skin round the stuffing, then fold the ham round to make a neat package.
- Place on an oiled baking tray, join down. Roast for 50 minutes.
- Serve whole, or cut a couple of slices off and stand the leg bone straight up. A simple pickle, relish or gravy would be great with this.

Wine note

A lovely old Rioja would work really well here – strangely, either red or white. Both have the earthy richness that this humble dish needs.

Autumn

Partridges in Red Cabbage

Cabbage has a natural affinity with partridge, and the little birds look ever so sweet nestling in the meltingly sweet red cabbage.

Serves 6
Preparation time: 30 minutes
Cooking time: 1½ hours

3 tablespoons olive oil
6 partridges
200g (7oz) streaky bacon, cut into lardons
1 red cabbage, shredded
grated zest of 1 orange *or* lemon
1 teaspoon juniper berries
pinch of ground mace
½ teaspoon salt
2 tablespoons brandy
125ml (4½floz) game stock
125ml (4½floz) white wine
freshly ground black pepper

- Preheat the oven to 150°C/300°F/Gas 2.
- Heat the oil in a non-stick frying pan. Add the partridges with the bacon lardons and brown lightly on all sides. Remove from the heat.
- Grease or oil an ovenproof dish and use half the cabbage to line the dish. Place the birds, breasts up, in the dish and scatter over the grated zest, juniper berries and bacon lardons. Sprinkle with the mace, the salt and pepper to taste. Cover with the rest of the cabbage and pour the liquids over the top.
- Cover with foil, put into the bottom half of the oven and cook for about 1½ hours.

Wine note

This is quite a robust dish and could take a mellow Chianti, a Côtes du Rhône or a light red Burgundy.

Autumn

Thai Roast Duck Curry

Although it sounds rather odd to cook the duck twice, this is a classic of Thai cuisine, influenced by the Chinese barbecue technique. You can wander through the Chinatown of Bangkok and see barbecued beasts hanging on stalls and in windows – everything from cuttlefish to chitterlings (pigs' intestines). Yellow curry paste can be bought in good supermarkets, delis and Thai food shops.

Serves 6 as part of a bigger meal
Preparation time: 30 minutes
Cooking time: 15 minutes

2 aubergines, about 600g (1lb 5oz) total
2 tablespoons yellow curry paste
2 tablespoons sunflower oil
400ml (14floz) coconut milk
1 roast duck
12 fresh lime leaves
15g (½oz) fresh coriander leaves
juice of 2 limes
salt and pepper

- Cut the aubergines into diamond shapes. The easiest way to do this is to top and tail the fruits then cut them into about 8 vertical wedges. Cut the outer 2cm (¾in) away from the spongy core, which you discard. Cut each of the strips on a diagonal to form diamond shapes. Sprinkle with salt and leave to drain for 20 minutes. Rinse and pat dry.
- Fry the curry paste in the oil in a saucepan. When the aroma starts to develop add the coconut milk and bring to the boil. Add the aubergines and simmer for 7–8 minutes.
- Meanwhile, chop the duck into bite-sized pieces using a cleaver. Traditionally the skin and bone are not removed, but you may wish to discard either or both.
- Add the duck and the lime leaves to the sauce and heat through for 5 minutes.
- Stir in the coriander and then the lime juice to sharpen the taste, and serve with rice.

Autumn

Pheasant Breast with Sausage and Pecan Stuffing, Thyme Jus

The breast meat of pheasant can be dry, especially later in the season, and this stuffing ensures a rich, juicy result. Nuts, sausages and game mean autumn to me and they work so well together. Pheasants bought in feather can easily be jointed and skinned.

Serves 8
Preparation time: 45 minutes
Cooking time: 35 minutes

100g (3½oz) onion, finely diced
3½ tablespoons olive oil
1 garlic clove, finely chopped
1 egg
3 best-quality Italian pork sausages, removed from their skins
200g (7oz) pecans, roughly chopped
2 teaspoons fresh thyme leaves *or* 1 teaspoon dried thyme

8 pheasant breasts
16 slices Speck *or* 8 slices Parma ham
16 field *or* flat mushrooms, peeled and stalks removed
salt and pepper

For the jus
250ml (8½floz) Red Wine Jus (see page 232)
1 tablespoon fresh thyme leaves

- Preheat the oven to 200°C/400°F/Gas 6.
- Fry the onion in 1 tablespoon of the oil until translucent but not coloured. Add the garlic and continue frying for 30 seconds. Remove from the heat.
- Beat the egg in a large bowl with a pinch of salt and generous grindings of black pepper. Add the sausage meat, pecans and onion and mix well. Add the thyme leaves, with another grinding of black pepper, and set aside.

- With a sharp knife, cut a pocket in each of the pheasant breasts. Stuff with one-eighth of the sausage and pecan mixture.
- For each pheasant breast, lay 2 slices of Speck, or 1 of Parma ham, slightly overlapping, on the work surface. Place the breasts on the ham and fold the ham round to make a neat package. Wrap each package in oiled foil and twist the ends to secure.
- Roast for 35 minutes. When done, leave to rest for 5–10 minutes.
- Meanwhile, combine the Red Wine Jus and thyme and leave to infuse.
- Brush the mushrooms with the remaining olive oil, then arrange them in a roasting tin or baking tray. Season with salt and pepper. Put into the oven with the pheasant for the last 12–15 minutes of the roasting time.
- To serve, unwrap the pheasant and slice into rounds. Arrange the pheasant and mushrooms on warmed plates flooded with the *jus*.

Winter

Pheasant with Calvados and Apples

Pheasant can be a little dry and is best partnered with a rich sauce, as in this example with apples. The Normans cooked pork in this way, using their local apple and dairy products, and the method works equally well with pheasant. Breast meat is often available cheaply later in the season, as the breasts can be cut off and skinned, rather than plucking the whole bird. The same is true of wood pigeon, as the rest of the bird has little to recommend it.

Serves 6
Preparation time: 15 minutes
Cooking time: 20 minutes

2 teaspoons butter
2 teaspoons olive oil
6 pheasant breasts
3 shallots, finely chopped
6 small cooking apples, peeled and cut into wedges
1 tablespoon Calvados *or* cider brandy
500ml (17floz) cider
250ml (8½floz) double cream
15g (½oz) fresh tarragon, leaves picked off
salt and pepper

- Preheat the oven to 190°C/375°F/Gas 5.
- Heat the butter and oil in a frying pan and fry the breasts until browned, about 2 minutes on each side. Transfer to a baking tray and cook in the oven for about 12 minutes or until done.
- Meanwhile, fry the shallots in the fat remaining in the frying pan until soft and browned. Using a slotted spoon, remove the shallots to a plate, and add the apples to the pan. Cook until soft, turning to cook all sides evenly; remove and reserve.
- Deglaze the frying pan with the Calvados. Add the cider and reduce by two-thirds. Return the shallots to the pan, with the cream and reduce until syrupy.
- Reheat the breasts and apples in the sauce, stir in the tarragon. Season, serve.

Winter

Velvet Chicken with Pineapple Rice

Velvet chicken is a Chinese dish I used for my series in Thailand, to show the versatility of ginger. The poaching of the chicken cooks the cornflour and does give a velvety texture. Strange but effective. Be sure your cooked rice is no older than a day and that it has been refrigerated – there is a particularly nasty strain of food poisoning that lives in rice, best avoided!

Serves 6 as part of a Chinese meal, with other dishes
Preparation time: 15 minutes
Cooking time: 8 minutes

2 large skinless boneless chicken breasts, cut into 1cm (½in) slices
cornflour for coating
3 tablespoons vegetable oil
a 2.5cm (1in) piece of fresh ginger, peeled and cut into matchsticks
200g (7oz) mange-touts
4 spring onions, cut into 2cm (¾in) pieces
100ml (3½floz) chicken stock
1 tablespoon light soy sauce
juice of 1 lime

For the pineapple rice
1 pineapple
2 tablespoons sunflower oil
3 garlic cloves, crushed
a 2cm (¾in) piece of fresh ginger, cut into matchsticks
1 medium onion, finely chopped
450g (1lb) cold cooked rice
2 tablespoons light soy sauce
1 tablespoon dark soy sauce
2 tablespoons chicken stock
2 tablespoons chopped fresh coriander

- Cut the pineapple in half lengthways and scoop out the flesh, to leave two attractive boats in which to serve the rice. Remove the core from the pineapple flesh and chop the pineapple into 2cm (¾in) dice. Set aside.
- Bring a pan of water to the simmer. Dust the chicken slices well with cornflour, then poach in the water for 3 minutes; remove and drain.

- To prepare the rice, heat a wok and add the oil, then sauté the garlic, ginger and onion until they soften. Add the rice and stir for 1 minute or until hot. Add the soy sauces and stock and mix well. Toss through the diced pineapple and coriander. Remove from the wok and keep warm.
- To finish the chicken, heat the oil in the wok, add the chicken and ginger and stir-fry until it is starting to become opaque. Add the mange-touts and spring onions and cook for a further 1 minute. Add the stock and soy sauce. Cook for 1 more minute, then squeeze in the lime juice.
- Serve the chicken immediately, with the pineapple rice piled into the pineapple boats.

Chef's tip

There is an old wives' tale about testing a pineapple for ripeness by pulling leaves out of the top crown. However, the best way to test for ripeness is to smell the fruit. If you can smell its perfume, it is probably ripe. The same is true of melons.

Winter

Chicken Fricassee with Lemons and Rosemary

When I cooked at the Canal Brasserie this was a staple – a good way to use up the thighs from chickens that had been used for supremes. It was known by all as 'chix frix' and remains a favourite. Chicken thighs are often overlooked, but, in fact, they have twice the flavour and succulence of the breasts. Ideal for barbecuing, they are also perfect for slow cooking on the hob.

Serves 6
Preparation time: 10 minutes
Cooking time: 55 minutes

2 tablespoons vegetable oil
15g ($\frac{1}{2}$oz) butter
12 chicken thighs
1 sprig of fresh rosemary *or* 1 teaspoon dried rosemary
3 garlic cloves, peeled
6 tablespoons dry white wine
2 tablespoons freshly squeezed lemon juice
thinly pared lemon zest, with none of the white pith, cut into 6 thin julienne strips
salt and freshly ground black pepper

- Choose a large pan that can accommodate all the chicken thighs without overlapping. Put in the oil and butter, set over a moderately high heat and, when the butter foam begins to subside, put in the chicken, skin side down. Brown the chicken on both sides, then add the rosemary and garlic. Season with salt and pepper. Cook for 6–7 minutes, turning the chicken from time to time.
- Add the wine and let it bubble at a brisk simmer for about 20 seconds, then adjust the heat to cook at a very slow simmer. Cover the pan so that the lid is slightly askew. Cook for about 45 minutes or until the chicken thighs feel very tender when prodded with a fork and the meat comes easily off the bone.

While it's cooking, check the liquid in the pan from time to time. If it becomes insufficient, replenish with 2 or 3 tablespoons of water.
- When the chicken is done, remove from the heat and transfer the pieces to a warm serving platter, using a slotted spoon or spatula. Tip the pan and spoon off almost all of the fat. Add the lemon juice and lemon zest. Return the pan to a moderately low heat and simmer, using a wooden spoon to scrape loose the cooking residues from the bottom and sides of the pan.
- Pour the cooking juices over the chicken and serve at once.

Wine note

The acidity of the lemon and the mellowness of the oil would suggest a citrusy but mouth-filling Semillon from Australia.

Winter

Tarragon Chicken with Mushroom 'Boxes'

This easy supper dish is a perfect example of how mundane ingredients can be made really exciting, simply by treating them with a little flair. The inspiration is the traditional French dish of chicken with truffles. It doesn't matter which mushrooms you use to fill the boxes, although a greater variety gives a more dramatic – and delicious – result. For a vegetarian main course, you could make bigger mushroom boxes and serve them with the spinach and a salad (leaving out the chicken, of course).

Serves 6
Preparation time: 30 minutes
Cooking time: 50 minutes

150g (5½oz) butter, softened
4 tablespoons fresh tarragon leaves
6 chicken supremes
2 tablespoons olive oil
300g (10½oz) fresh spinach leaves
salt and pepper

For the mushroom boxes
6 cubes of bread *or* brioche, each
    8 × 8cm (3¼ × 3¼in) and 6cm
    (2½in) thick
85g (3oz) butter, melted
200g (7oz) mixed mushrooms, sliced
2 tablespoons olive oil

4 tablespoons double cream

- Preheat the oven to 180°C/350°F/Gas 4.
- First make the boxes. Hollow out the cubes of bread from the top to make box shapes. Brush them with melted butter and arrange on a baking tray. Bake for 25 minutes or until golden brown. Remove and set aside to cool. Leave the oven on.
- Mash the softened butter with the tarragon leaves and season with salt and pepper. Divide the tarragon butter into 6 portions. Gently work your fingers under the skin on each chicken supreme to loosen it and make a pocket. Ease in

a portion of tarragon butter. (As the chicken cooks, the butter will melt, leaving the tarragon behind to scent and flavour the flesh. The butter acts as a basting agent to keep the breast juicy and succulent.)
- Heat 1 tablespoon of the oil in a roasting pan, add the chicken supremes, skin side up, and brown the bottom side briefly. Transfer the pan to the oven and roast for about 20 minutes. To test if the chicken is cooked, pierce the meat near the wing bone; the juices that run out should be clear, not at all pink.
- While the chicken is roasting, fry the mushrooms in the oil until they are beginning to soften and have exuded liquid. Cook until the liquid evaporates, then add the cream and stir. Bubble slowly for 5 minutes to thicken. Remove from the heat and keep warm.
- When the chicken is cooked, remove from the oven and allow it to rest while you cook the spinach. Heat the remaining tablespoon oil in a frying pan and add the spinach and 4 tablespoons water. Cook over a medium-high heat, turning and stirring constantly, for 2 minutes or until the spinach is wilted and tender and all excess water has evaporated.
- To serve, divide the spinach among individual plates and place the chicken on top. Fill the boxes with the mushrooms and set one on each plate. Alternatively, all the components can be arranged on a large platter and served from this at table.

Wine note

The earthy mushroominess and herbal nature of the tarragon suggest a good solid white Burgundy such as a Meursault or a Montagny. The most memorable Meursault I have ever had was at the office of Louis Jadot in Beaune over lunch with the winemaker, Jacques. It was the '79 and was fantastic.

Winter

Stir-fry of Duck and Scallops

The richness of the duck and the sweetness of the scallops work very well together. Be sure to get the wok very hot to start with, to achieve a lovely caramelized colour and flavour for both the two principles. You could add a few mange-touts, but I rather like the whiteness of the bean sprouts mirroring the scallops' opalescence.

Serves 2
Preparation time: 10 minutes
Cooking time: 5 minutes

1 Barbary duck breast, trimmed of excess surrounding fat
2 tablespoons sunflower oil
6 fresh, fat scallops, without corals
2 garlic cloves, finely chopped
1 tablespoon black bean sauce
3 tablespoons chicken stock
1 teaspoon cornflour
100g (3½oz) bean sprouts

- Score the skin and fat of the duck breasts in a cross-hatch fashion, about 5mm (¼in) per square, then cut each breast across into 5mm (¼in) slices.
- Heat a wok to smoking point, then add the oil. Swirl it around the wok to coat. Throw in the scallops, which should sear on contact. Cook for 1 minute – this should be enough to cook them without making them rubbery. Remove to a warm plate and reserve.
- Add the duck slices to the hot wok (you may need a little more oil) and stir-fry for 1 minute. Add the garlic, black bean sauce and 2 tablespoons of the stock. Turn the duck slices quickly to coat and cook for a further 30 seconds.
- Mix the cornflour with the remaining stock, add to the wok and cook until the whole mixture is glossy.
- Return the scallops to the wok together with any released juices and the bean sprouts. Turn to mix thoroughly, then serve immediately.

Winter

Stress-free Christmas Turkey

Almost all families agonize over Christmas, and it's no wonder, given all the organization and co-ordination that is needed. By taking the festive bird apart not only do you get succulent white meat but also very easy-to-carve dark meat. The undercarriage can be made into stock the night before, and you don't need to get up at 3am to put the wretched thing in the oven! I spend my Christmases on an estate in Northamptonshire, with friends who are deeply traditional and won't let me attack the sacrosanct turkey, but I find this ideal for all the other Christmas meals I cook. I can't recommend it highly enough.

Serves 16
Preparation time: 30 minutes
Cooking time: 3 hours

a 7.2kg (16lb) turkey, cut into a breast joint and 2 boned legs, with bones, carcass and giblets for stock (ask your butcher to do this, but give him plenty of notice)

For the stuffing
200g (7oz) vacuum-packed chestnuts, roughly chopped
finely pared zest of 2 oranges, cut into fine strips (or taken off with a citrus zester)
6 fresh lime leaves, very finely shredded
2 streaky bacon rashers, chopped
25g (scant 1oz) butter
2 tablespoons chopped fresh oregano
1 egg, lightly beaten
2 garlic cloves, finely chopped
freshly ground black pepper

For the gravy
2 tablespoons plain flour
100ml (3½floz) Madeira

- Made a stock from the turkey giblets, bones and undercarriage of the carcass.
- Preheat the oven to 180°C/350°F/Gas 4.

Poultry & Feathered Game

- Mix the stuffing ingredients together and use to stuff the boned turkey legs. Roll them up from a long side and use fine string to tie each of these 'sausages' 7–8 times along the length.
- Put the stuffed legs and the breast joint in a roasting tin. Roast for 10 minutes for each 450g (1lb) of the original weight of the whole bird, e.g. if the turkey weighed 7.2kg (16lb), the legs and breast joint will take 2 hours 40 minutes. Baste with the turkey stock a few times during roasting, and cover the breast joint with foil if it starts to darken too much.
- When the cooking time has elapsed, test for doneness and then remove from the tin and leave to rest for 20–30 minutes.
- Meanwhile, make the gravy. Pour off the excess fat from the tin and add the flour. Stir over a moderate heat until cooked to a light brown. Add the Madeira and 600ml (1 pint) of the turkey stock and cook, stirring, until thickened. Season with salt and pepper.
- Return the stuffed turkey legs to the oven to reheat for 5 minutes before serving.
- To carve, remove the two breasts from the breast bone and slice. Remove the strings from the stuffed legs and neatly slice into pinwheel rounds. Serve with the gravy and traditional trimmings.

Wine note

Turkey is not best paired with great claret, but that is what I always seem to get to drink with it. It's Christmas, so have what you like!

MEAT

Spring

Saddle of Lamb stuffed with Spinach and Shiitakes

The leaner cuts of lamb, like all red meat, are best cooked underdone so they retain all their flavour and succulence. This is a great example of rare lamb in quite a grand setting. Get your butcher to bone out a saddle and you've got the smartest dinner dish, good enough to impress Hyacinth Bucket herself! Serve with Pommes Fondants (see Beef Fillet with Red Wine Jus and Wild Mushrooms, page 163).

Serves 6–8
Preparation time: 30 minutes
Cooking time: 45 minutes

a 2.25kg (5lb) saddle of lamb, boned
Dijon mustard
100ml (3½fl oz) vegetable oil
fresh chervil to garnish
Red Wine Jus (see page 232) or gravy to serve

For the stuffing
6 lamb's kidneys
2 shallots, finely diced
50g (scant 2oz) unsalted butter
200g (7oz) fresh shiitake mushrooms, cut into 5mm (¼in) dice
100ml (3½floz) port
600g (1lb 5oz) fresh spinach
1 egg, beaten
salt and pepper

- Preheat the oven to 200°C/400°F/Gas 6.
- To prepare the stuffing, skin the kidneys and remove all the veins. Cut in half, discard the core and all the fat and cut into small dice. Sweat the shallots in the butter until golden brown. Throw in the kidney dice and allow to colour nicely, then add the mushrooms and fry for 1 more minute. Add the port and reduce until almost completely evaporated. Leave to cool.
- Remove any tough stalks from the spinach. Steam until wilted. Allow to cool, then squeeze dry and chop roughly. Mix the spinach into the kidney and mushroom mixture together with the egg and plenty of salt and pepper.

- Trim any excess fat from the lamb. Place it on the work surface, skin side down. Trim the flaps and season the meat. Spread it all over with a little Dijon mustard. Put the stuffing inside, then fold over the two fillets and flaps on top and roll up. Tie with string.
- Heat the oil in a roasting tin and sear the rolled saddle all over. Transfer to the oven and roast for 45 minutes. When cooked allow to rest for 15 minutes.
- Carve into 2cm (¾in) slices and serve garnished with chervil, with Red Wine Jus or gravy.

Wine note

A splendid dish like this deserves a cracking red Burgundy such as a Morey St Denis or a heavier one like Pommard.

Spring

Rabbit on Watercress with a Port Sauce

Peter bunny is sadly little used in Britain, possibly due to his fluffy image and memories of Watership Down. *Elsewhere in Europe all manner of cooking methods create delicacies from the tender and tasty meat of rabbit. In this dish, which I did for* Masterchef, *the fillet, which resembles chicken, is simply roasted, while the legs are given a darker flavour. The mushrooms, with their juicy earthiness, are just made for the rabbit. What a perfect afternoon could be spent in the country harvesting both!*

Serves 6
Preparation time: 10 minutes
Cooking time: 30 minutes

3 wild rabbits, jointed into saddles and hind legs, the carcass and kidneys retained
2 tablespoons sunflower oil
25g (scant 1oz) butter
240ml (8floz) port
500ml (17floz) clear chicken stock

For the garnish
6 large field mushrooms
sunflower oil
18 shallots, peeled
45g (1½oz) butter
500g (1lb 2oz) watercress leaves
6 sprigs of fresh chervil
salt and pepper

- Preheat the oven to 225°C/425°F/Gas 7.
- Chop the rabbit carcasses. Heat 4 teaspoons of the oil and the butter in a heavy roasting tin and fry the carcasses until browned. Remove and reserve. Brown the rabbit joints in the hot fat remaining in the tin. Return the carcasses to the tin, then transfer to the oven and roast for 12 minutes.
- Remove the saddles and keep warm while the carcasses and legs continue to roast for 10 minutes.

- Meanwhile, sprinkle the field mushrooms with a little oil, season and roast for 10 minutes; keep warm. Put the shallots and 15g (½oz) butter in another small roasting tin, season and roast for 8 minutes or so; keep warm.
- Remove the legs from the roasting tin and keep warm with the saddles. Pour the oil from the roasting tin, then set over a moderate heat and deglaze with the port. Reduce by half. Add the stock and reduce by half again.
- Meanwhile, melt the remaining butter in a small saucepan and sweat the watercress for 2–3 minutes. Season. Remove the fillets from the saddles and carve each against the grain into about 6 slices.
- Arrange the watercress to the side of 6 warmed plates and top each with a sliced rabbit fillet and then a leg. Put 3 shallots on top of a roasted mushroom on the other side of each plate. Quickly flash-fry the rabbit kidneys in the remaining oil. Finish the shallots with a kidney and then a sprig of chervil. Strain the sauce through a fine sieve and pour around the rabbit. Serve.

Wine note

Game and red Burgundy work so well together. The mushroomy characteristics in this dish suggest a Chambolle-Musigny or perhaps a Rully.

Spring

Loin of Lamb with Artichokes

This is an ideal main course for a smart barbecue as there is plenty of pre-planning possible and the execution is very easy. The loin of lamb is quite expensive, but is completely lean and very tasty. It comes from the saddle and is really the only part of the lamb that should be cooked pink. If overcooked, it will be dry and tasteless, whereas most lamb benefits from long, slow cooking. You can substitute bottled artichokes for the fresh, but rinse them really well, dry and dress with excellent quality olive oil to revive them before serving. This dish makes no sauce, so serve with Root Vegetable Gratin (see page 196), with dauphinoise potatoes or another juicy accompaniment.

Serves 4
Preparation time: 35 minutes
Cooking time: 15 minutes

1 saddle of lamb, trimmed into loin fillets (ask your butcher to do this)
4 tablespoons olive oil
2 sprigs of fresh rosemary
6 courgettes (3 yellow and 3 green), cut into long julienne, like spaghetti
juice of 1 lemon
4 large *or* 8 small fresh globe artichokes
2 lemons, cut into quarters

- Marinate the lamb fillets in half of the oil with the rosemary for a couple of hours.
- Mix the courgette 'spaghetti' with the remaining oil and the lemon juice and set aside. (This will 'cook' the courgettes, so they are soft enough to be formed into skeins later.)
- Prepare the artichokes by removing the coarse outside leaves and then cutting across, just above the choke, and peeling off the remaining leaves; keep dipping into a large pan of water acidulated with the quartered lemons to prevent discoloration. Peel the stalks and remove the hairy choke from the middle. As each artichoke is prepared, put it into the acidulated water. When all are in the

pan, bring to the boil. Remove from the heat and allow to cool in the water. Before serving, drain and trim off any blackened or discoloured parts.
- Grill the lamb on a barbecue or ridged cast-iron grill pan for about 4 minutes on each side. Alternatively, brown in a pan and then roast in the oven preheated to 200°C/400°F/Gas 6 for 7 minutes. Cover and leave to rest for 5 minutes, to relax and allow the juices to go back into the meat.
- Slice the fillets and serve with skeins of the courgette spaghetti and the artichokes.

Wine note

A gutsy Californian red, such as a Ridge Zinfandel, would be ideal with the flavours here.

Spring

Spice-crusted Pork Fillet, Lentil Salad and Avocado

Pork is widely used in Mexico and Asia, whereas it has been slightly ignored in a great deal of western Europe. Pigs are now bred to be far leaner than was previously the case, and thus their meat is not as unhealthy as one might think. The fillet or tenderloin is a favourite cut for the health-conscious and is widely available.

Serves 6
Preparation time: 30 minutes
Cooking time: 20 minutes

For the pork
1kg (2¼lb) pork fillets
1 teaspoon ground cumin
1 teaspoon paprika
1 teaspoon chilli powder
1 teaspoon dried thyme
1 teaspoon turmeric
6 sprigs of fresh coriander to garnish

For the lentil salad
250g (9oz) Puy lentils
1 red onion, finely diced
60ml (2floz) olive oil
juice of 2 limes
3 tablespoons chopped fresh coriander
6 slices Parma ham

For the avocado sauce
2 avocados
2 garlic cloves, peeled
240ml (8floz) double cream
120ml (4floz) milk
juice of 2 limes
salt and pepper

- Preheat the oven to 200°C/400°F/Gas 6.
- Cook the lentils in unsalted water for 20 minutes.
- Meanwhile, trim the pork of all fat and sinew and the very thin ends, then divide into 6 portions. Mix together all the spices with 1 teaspoon each of salt and pepper on a large plate. Roll the pork in the mixture. Heat a heavy-bottomed frying pan and blacken the pork on all sides. Transfer to a roasting

tin and cook in the oven for 12 minutes. Test for doneness, then leave to rest for 5 minutes.
- To make the avocado sauce, blend the flesh of the avocado with the other ingredients and season.
- When the lentils are cooked, drain and rinse. Add the red onion and dress with the oil, lime juice, coriander and seasoning. Line 6 ramekins or teacups with the Parma ham and fill with the lentil salad. Invert one in the centre of each plate.
- Carve the pork and arrange around the lentil salad. Garnish with the coriander sprigs and surround with a ribbon of avocado sauce.

Chef's tip

To ripen fruit or avocados, place in a paper bag with a banana. The banana releases ethylene as it ripens, and this speeds the ripening of the other fruit.

Spring

Authentic Pork Vindaloo

Real vindaloo is not the travesty of 'I-can-take-more-chilli-than-you-can' curries one normally thinks of, but is acually a delicious dish of a far finer pedigree. Vindaloo, or vindalho, is a Portugese-Indian dish once eaten by the merchants of places such as Diu and Goa. The flavourings were garlic (alhos) and wine (vinho) vinegar. The vinegar acted as a preservative and allowed the pork dish to be eaten over a couple of days.

Serves 4–6
Preparation time: 20 minutes plus overnight marinating
Cooking time: 1 hour

1kg (2¼lb) boneless pork from the shoulder, cut into 5cm (2in) cubes
1¼ teaspoons salt
4 tablespoons red wine vinegar
3 tablespoons vegetable oil
3–4 garlic cloves, lightly crushed
3 medium-sized onions, thinly sliced
2 large tomatoes, chopped
6 fresh green chillies, sliced in half lengthways
1 teaspoon sugar

For the spice paste
4–10 dried red chillies
1 tablespoon bright red paprika
½ teaspoon cumin seeds
a 7.5cm (3in) cinnamon stick, broken up into smaller pieces
10–15 cloves
½ teaspoon black peppercorns
5–6 cardamom pods
10–12 garlic cloves, peeled
a 2.5cm (1in) piece of fresh ginger, peeled and coarsely chopped
½ teaspoon turmeric
2 tablespoons red wine vinegar

- Sprinkle the pork with 1 teaspoon of the salt and 3 tablespoons of the vinegar. Rub in well, then set aside to marinate for 2–3 hours.
- To make the spice paste, combine the dried red chillies, paprika, cumin seeds, cinnamon, cloves, peppercorns and cardamom pods in a clean coffee grinder or spice grinder and grind as finely as possible. Put the garlic cloves and ginger in a blender together with the turmeric and vinegar. Blend well. Add the dry ground spices to the garlic mixture and blend again to make a paste.

- Rub the pork cubes with half of the spice paste. Cover and refrigerate overnight. Cover and refrigerate the remaining spice paste.
- The next day, heat the oil in a wide, preferably non-stick pan over moderately high heat. When hot, put in the crushed garlic. Stir and fry until they begin to pick up a little colour. Add the onions and continue to fry until browned. Add the tomatoes and 3 of the fresh green chillies. Stir for 1 minute. Add the remaining spice paste, the sugar and the remaining tablespoon of vinegar. Stir and fry until the mixture begins to brown a little.
- Add the marinated pork and all the spice paste clinging to it. Turn the heat to moderately low and cook, stirring, until the pork begins to exude its own liquid.
- Add 300ml (10floz) of water and the remaining salt and bring to the boil. Cover, turn the heat to low and simmer gently for about 40 minutes until the meat is tender and the sauce has thickened somewhat. If necessary, towards the end of cooking raise the heat to reduce the sauce to a medium-thick consistency.
- Add the remaining 3 fresh green chillies and stir once, then serve.

Summer

Butterflied Leg of Lamb with Juniper, Walnut Oil and Oregano

Barbecues are almost a religion in New Zealand, as is our reverence for lamb. A whole leg, boned and flattened, is the perfect thing to cook over slow coals to feed 10–12 people. A starter can easily be cooked first, without draining out too much heat from the fire. Any good butcher will bone the leg for you, or you can do it yourself using a little patience and a sharp knife. The flavours of juniper, walnut and oregano are redolent of the south of France. To enhance this, soak some thyme sprigs in water and add to the coals. When I barbecue in Italy I always gather dried fennel stems and add them to the coals to give an aniseedy tang to meat and fish. The lamb needs to rest rather well after cooking to become tender, and can then be simply and deliciously dressed by mixing the released juices into some home-made mayo, as in the following beef recipe.

Serves 8–10
Preparation time: 5 minutes plus overnight marinating
Cooking time: about 40 minutes

a 2.25–3kg (5–6½lb) leg of lamb, boned and butterflied
100ml (3½floz) walnut oil
12 juniper berries
15g (½oz) fresh oregano leaves
3 garlic cloves, finely chopped
freshly ground black pepper

- Marinate the lamb overnight in the oil with the remaining ingredients.
- Barbecue over a low charcoal fire, not too near the coals, for about 20 minutes each side, skin side down first. (The secret to good barbecues is to ensure that the charcoal fire is well developed rather than flaming, which would scorch the exterior of the lamb and leave the interior raw.)
- Allow to rest well before carving.

Summer

Fillet of Beef with Summer Salad

I devised this dish for a buffet given by great clients at their country house in Wiltshire. When I first met Lady Tanlaw we ran through the event and the kitchen, and she ended by asking if I needed anything else. I replied that as she'd booked me, I didn't know if her husband was a knight or a peer, and so didn't know how to address him. 'Oh, it's Lord Tanlaw,' she exclaimed, at which point the peer in point came into the kitchen and announced 'Oh, call me Simon, unless anybody terribly important is listening, then call me M'Lord!' We've been firm friends ever since.

Serves 12
Preparation time: 30 minutes
Cooking time: 40–60 minutes

1 fillet of finest beef, trimmed to the thickest section without the tail
3 tablespoons olive oil
500g (1lb 2oz) frozen broad beans, thawed, drained and skinned
2 x 425g (15oz) cans artichoke hearts, drained, *or* their equivalent of cooked fresh artichokes
500g (1lb 2oz) asparagus, trimmed and blanched for 1½ minutes in salted water
15g (½oz) fresh tarragon, leaves only
30g (1oz) fresh chervil, in small sprigs
½ quantity Basic Mayonnaise (see page 230)
salt and pepper

- Preheat the oven to 240°C/475°F/Gas 9 or its highest setting.
- Allow the fillet to come to room temperature. Heat the oil in a heavy roasting tin until very hot, then sear the fillet on all sides until dark brown. Transfer to the oven and roast for 40 minutes for pink, 60 minutes for well done. (This is much better served pink as the meat retains its juiciness.)
- Remove the fillet from the oven, cover with foil and a tea cloth and allow to rest in a warm place for 10 minutes.

- Meanwhile, mix the vegetables and herbs together in a bowl and pile on to a serving platter.
- Carve the beef into thick slices and pile on to the vegetable salad. Mix the released beef juices into the mayonnaise. Season the beef and salad, then drizzle over the mayonnaise.

Wine note

A Cabernet Sauvignon from New Zealand, with its minty, slightly green characteristics, would be superb.

SUMMER

Mexican-style Loin of Pork

I once had a holiday in the city of Oaxaca in Mexico, where this dish is a speciality. The central market was a warren of stalls with sacks of many types of dried chillies. The dried chillies needed for this recipe are marketed by the Cool Chile Company, in many supermarkets or directly from them by mail order. You could make twice the quantity of sauce and serve some separately.

Serves 10
Preparation time: 20 plus at least 6 hours marinating
Cooking time: about 3 hours

500ml (17floz) freshly squeezed orange juice
6 ancho chillies, seeds and membranes removed
8 pasilla chillies, seeds and membranes removed
¼ onion
90ml (3floz) cider vinegar
10 garlic cloves
1 teaspoon dried thyme
3 cloves
1 teaspoon ground cumin
1 tablespoon dried oregano
a 5cm (2in) cinnamon stick
3 allspice berries
2 tablespoons coarse salt
1 loin of pork, about 3 kg (6½lb)
30g (1oz) lard

- In a small saucepan, heat half of the orange juice until warm. Toast the chillies in a cast-iron frying pan or griddle, then let them soak in the warm orange juice for 20 minutes. Transfer the chillies and orange juice to a blender, add the onion and vinegar, and purée. Set aside.
- In a mortar grind the garlic with the thyme, cloves, cumin, oregano, cinnamon, allspice and salt. Add the puréed chillies and stir well. Add enough of the remaining orange juice to dilute the mixture until it has the consistency of yogurt.
- Use a fork to pierce the loin of pork all over. Place in an ovenproof dish and cover with the chilli and orange sauce. Cover and marinate in the refrigerator for at least 6 hours, or preferably overnight. Turn occasionally.
- About 2 hours before roasting, remove the loin of pork from the refrigerator and smear lightly with the lard. Let stand in the sauce at room temperature.

MEAT

- Preheat the oven to 180°C/350°F/Gas 4.
- Cover the ovenproof dish with foil. Roast for 2 hours, basting frequently with the pan juices. Turn the meat over, cover again and roast for a further 1 hour or so.
- When the meat can be easily pierced with a fork, turn the oven temperature up to 230°C/450°F/Gas 8. Uncover the meat and roast for 5–10 minutes or until browned, being careful not to let it burn. Leave to stand for 15 minutes before cutting into thin slices.

> ## Wine note
> *This dish does have quite a kick, so either serve lager or fruity cocktails, or a zesty white such as Pinot Blanc or white Bordeaux.*

SUMMER

Pressed Ox Tongue, My Grandmother's Way

When I was a child in New Zealand, cold meats, salads and barbecues were everyday fare. One of my favourite things was pressed tongue, either tiny sweet lamb's tongues or big and more seriously flavoured ox tongue. My grandmother is a master of both and, although she now seldom cooks, on my last visit home she produced this fine dish as a treat for me. I assume it was a treat meant for me because few other people got any!

Serves 10
Preparation time: 25 minutes plus overnight setting
Cooking time: 3 hours

1 ox tongue, about 1kg (2¼lb), pickled
1 teaspoon black peppercorns
2 onions, studded with cloves
4 sachets powdered gelatine, each 10g (¼oz)
4 hard-boiled eggs, shelled
6 egg whites, plus the egg shells, to clarify the stock
salt

- Put the tongue in a pan of water and bring to the boil, then drain and return to the pan. Cover again with cold water and add the peppercorns, 2 teaspoons of salt and the onions. Bring to the boil. Simmer for 3 hours or until the tongue feels tender when pierced at the thick end. Leave to cool in the cooking liquid.
- Remove the tongue (reserve the stock). Peel away the skin and any tiny bones at the base. Set aside.
- If the stock is not perfectly clear, you can clarify it. Measure 1.5 litres (2¾ pints) of the stock, return to the pan and bring to a simmer. Beat the egg whites to a peak. Pour them into the stock, with the egg shells, and stir. The whites and shells should float to the surface, taking the impurities from the stock with them. Ladle the stock over the whites until it is clear, then make a well in the whites and ladle out the clear stock. Measure out 1 litre (1¾ pints) and keep warm. Discard the rest of the stock, and the egg whites.

- Soften the gelatine in a little of the warm stock, then stir into the remainder.
- Place the tongue in the bottom of a 2 litre (3½ pint) basin and surround with the whole eggs. Pour over the stock. Refrigerate, weighted, overnight.
- To serve, unmould and cut into thick slices. Serve with mustard and crusty bread.

Autumn

Lamb Shanks in Red Wine with Champ

I once ran a fantastic restaurant in Auckland called Vinnies, which was then small and BYO (bring your own alcohol). It's still there, now licenced and expanded, but just as good. The chefs/patrons, Prue and David, are stunning judges of flavour (and character!) and the house favourite was lamb shanks (this was in the days when lamb shanks were unheard of). Delicious and good value, they're a winter warmer of the first order. Like pig's trotters, the shank bones give a wonderful gelatinous quality to the sauce. Any leftover sauce would make a great addition to bangers and mash, lifting them to ambrosial levels.

Serves 6
Preparation time: 30 minutes
Cooking time: 1½–2 hours

4 tablespoons sunflower oil
6 lamb shanks
360ml (12floz) red wine
2 carrots, each cut into 3
18 shallots, peeled
6 garlic cloves, peeled
a few sprigs of fresh thyme or rosemary
pared zest of 1 orange
black pepper

For the champ
1kg (2¼lb) white potatoes such as King Edwards, peeled
100g (3½oz) butter
300ml (10floz) milk, warmed
1 bunch spring onions, thinly sliced
salt and pepper

- Preheat the oven to 180°C/350°F/Gas 4.
- Heat the oil in a flameproof casserole or roasting tin that will snugly hold the shanks and brown them over a good heat. Remove and reserve.
- Pour off the fat from the casserole and deglaze with the red wine. Return the shanks to the casserole and add the vegetables and garlic. Tuck the herbs and orange zest under the lamb and season with black pepper. Add just enough

water to cover the lamb. Bring to the boil. Transfer to the oven and cook for 1½–2 hours, adding water from time to time as needed.
- To make the champ, put the potatoes into a pan of cold salted water, bring to the boil and cook until tender. Drain well and return to the pan.
- Crush the potatoes rather than mash them. Mix in the butter, milk and spring onions and season with salt and pepper. Keep warm.
- When the shanks are tender, remove and keep warm. Strain the juices and keep the shallots. Reduce the juices to a glossy glaze.
- Reheat the shanks and shallots in the sauce, then serve with the champ.

Wine note

It is a rare exception that claret suits lamb, and the richness of shanks is unlike any other part of the beast. A good 10-year-old claret, serious Rhône such as Côte Rôtie or a fabulous Shiraz such as Hensche would partner this very well.

Autumn

Pork with Juniper and Porcini

Autumn in Sienna brings mushrooms, lavender and juniper. This dish is adapted from a Marches recipe and encapsulates the late season in that sun-dappled land.

Serves 8
Preparation time: 30 minutes
Cooking time: 1½–2 hours

50g (scant 2oz) dried porcini
150ml (5floz) olive oil
1.35kg (3lb) boned pork shoulder, cubed
4 teaspoons chopped onion
4 teaspoons red wine vinegar
200ml (7floz) white wine
6 anchovy fillets, finely chopped

30 juniper berries
3 bay leaves, chopped if fresh and crumbled if dry
a few sprigs of fresh oregano *or* marjoram
1 fresh red chilli, finely chopped
black pepper

- Soak the porcini in 500ml (17floz) boiling water to rehydrate. Drain, reserving the water, and set aside. Filter the soaking water through a fine sieve lined with a tea cloth and reserve.
- Put the olive oil into a large flameproof casserole and, when hot, sauté the pork in batches until brown. Remove to a plate when done.
- Add the onion to the casserole and cook until soft and golden. Deglaze the casserole with the vinegar and wine.
- Return the meat to the casserole and add the porcini with their filtered liquid, the anchovies, juniper berries, bay leaves, herbs and chilli. Stir gently and reduce the flame to very low. Add a few grindings of black pepper. Seal the casserole tightly and cook for 1½–2 hours, checking twice for liquid.
- The pork is done if it feels tender when prodded with a fork. Tip away any excess fat and serve.

Autumn

Long-cooked Leg of Lamb in Red Wine

Lamb often needs to be very well cooked to release its flavour and not be bland. Added to this, the meat nearest the bone takes longer to cook, and rather than being appealingly rare is sometimes uncooked and jelly-like. So for the best results I suggest cooking the leg very well. This idea was passed to me by the very talented (and Michelin-starred) chef, Nick Nairn, who took it from Ronnie Rose. No matter how involved a pedigree, it's sensational. The foil must not be pierced so all the moisture and succulence is kept in, and the cooking juices, wine and butter can emulsify to become a gravy. The flavourings are entirely up to you, but I suggest garlic and thyme.

Serves 8
Preparation time: 10 minutes
Cooking time: 3 hours

a 3kg (6½lb) leg of lamb
100g (3½oz) butter
12 garlic cloves, peeled
3 sprigs of fresh thyme

2 onions, quartered
300ml (10floz) red wine
25g (scant 1oz) coarse salt, crushed
white pepper

- Preheat the oven to 190°C/375°F/Gas 5.
- Line a roasting tin with enough foil to fold over and cover the lamb. Place the leg in the tin.
- Melt the butter in a small saucepan, then bring it to the boil. Scatter the garlic cloves and thyme over the lamb and place the onion quarters around it. Pour on the red wine and sprinkle over the salt and pepper to taste. Lastly, pour the boiling butter over the lamb. Seal the foil parcel and cook in the oven for 3 hours.
- Remove from the oven and leave to rest for 30 minutes in a warm place.

- To serve, lift out the leg of lamb and carve. Divide all the onion and garlic pieces among the plates. Strain all the juices into a saucepan. Reheat if necessary and check for seasoning, then pour over the lamb.

Wine note

Rather strangely, the Cabernet Sauvignon grape comes to mind. There is a fab little winery very near my parents' house, called the McDonald vineyard, which was founded in 1897. It is on Church Road, next to the Mission vineyard, run by Marist brothers, and is the oldest in New Zealand, having been founded in 1864. The McDonald lot produce a Church Road Cabernet that is delicious. It must be a complete coincidence that it is co-run by Cordier who own my favourite claret, Gruaud-Larose.

Autumn

Wild Boar Sauce for Noodles

This is the most delicious treat, made with bits of the wild boar that would not be otherwise utilized. The flavour of wild boar can be quite strong, but the long slow cooking here takes care of any harshness. Any leftovers can be frozen for up to 6 months with no deterioration in flavour. In fact, a day's resting in the fridge allows the flavours to develop, so it's an ideal cook-ahead sauce. Allow 200g (7oz) of fresh noodles per person when serving this.

Serves 10
Preparation time: 20 minutes
Cooking time: 1½ hours

6 tablespoons extra virgin olive oil
100g (3½oz) pancetta, diced
55g (2oz) onion, finely chopped
55g (2oz) carrot, finely chopped
55g (2oz) celery, finely diced
2 garlic cloves, finely chopped
800g (1¾lb) wild boar meat, minced

2 sprigs of fresh rosemary
1 bouquet garni
bunch of parsley
240ml (8floz) tomato passata
½ wineglass dry white wine
salt and pepper

- Heat 4 tablespoons of the olive oil in a frying pan and fry the pancetta until lightly browned. Add the onion, carrot, celery and garlic and cook until they are soft and golden. Transfer the pancetta and the vegetables to a heavy flameproof casserole using a slotted spoon.
- Heat the remaining oil in the frying pan and fry the mince until golden. Add this to the casserole.
- Tie the rosemary in a muslin bag and add to the casserole with the bouquet garni, parsley, tomato passata and wine. Bring gently to the boil. Add just enough hot water to cover the meat, and season with salt and pepper. Reduce the heat, cover and cook gently for 1 hour.

- Remove the herbs and check the seasoning. Make sure the sauce is of a dense consistency (boil to reduce, if necessary).
- To serve, cook the noodles in abundant boiling water. Drain and serve with the sauce.

Wine note

This is the perfect dish to serve with my favourite Italian red, Amarone. Made from half-dried Valpolicella grapes in the Veneto, it has a bitter cherry sweetness and is nectar. The best are single vineyard versions from Masi. At 15 years they start to be really good. An excellent alternative is the Ripasso wine, which is good Valpolicella aged on the dregs of the Amarone to pick up extra flavour and depth.

Autumn

Pork Chops with Chestnuts and Sherry

Despite its fusty image, sherry remains very popular among serious wine drinkers. A glass of old oloroso dulce with Christmas pudding or half a bottle of chilled fino between friends are both fantastic ways to tantalize your tastebuds. The amontillado I suggest here has a richness that other wines don't have and partners chestnuts very well. If ever there was a reason to welcome cold weather, this is it!

Serves 4
Preparation time: 10 minutes
Cooking time: 20 minutes

4 pork chops, bone removed
15g ($\frac{1}{2}$oz) butter
1 tablespoon sunflower oil
1 small onion, finely chopped
4 tablespoons sherry (amontillado or oloroso are best)
120ml (4floz) chicken stock
120ml (4floz) double cream
250g (9oz) vacuum-packed chestnuts
1 teaspoon grain mustard

- Snip the skin on the chops 5 or 6 times so they will retain their shape during cooking. Melt the butter with the oil in a frying pan and, when bubbling, slip in the chops. Cook on a moderate heat, turning twice, for about 12 minutes. (To keep the flesh juicy, cook moderately fast rather than rapidly.) When done, remove the chops to a plate, cover with foil and leave to rest.
- Fry the onion in the fat remaining in the pan until translucent. Drain away the excess fat, then deglaze with the sherry. Reduce by half. Add the stock and reduce by half again. Add the cream to the pan and bubble until thick, adding the chestnuts and mustard after 3 minutes.
- When the sauce is almost done, return the chops to the pan with any released juices. Serve the chops with noodles or jacket potatoes and a salad.

Winter

Beef Fillet with Red Wine Jus and Wild Mushrooms

Fillet of beef is the ultimate for entertaining as it is luxurious but actually easy to prepare. The sauce can be made in advance, as can the garnish, and the beef takes very little time to cook. Each of the slices of fillet is best served on pommes fondants or a small rosti to absorb the delicious juices that will flow.

Serves 8–10
Preparation time: 20 minutes
Cooking time: 40–60 minutes

1 fillet of beef, trimmed of all sinew, fat and its tail, at room temperature
3 tablespoons olive oil
Red Wine Jus (see page 232)

For the pommes fondants
8 baking potatoes
100g (3½oz) butter

salt and pepper

For the garnish
300g (10½oz) fresh chanterelles *or* girolles, cleaned
25g (scant 1oz) butter
2 teaspoons olive oil
8–10 sprigs of fresh chervil

- To prepare the pommes fondants, peel the potatoes and shape into neat rounds or ovals 2–3cm (¾–1¼in) thick. Keep in water until ready to use, then drain.
- Preheat the oven to 200°C/400°F/Gas 6. Select a roasting tin just big enough to accommodate the potato pieces comfortably and smear it with the butter. Sit the potatoes on the butter and season. Add enough water to the tin to make a 5mm (¼in) layer over the butter.
- Bake for 30–45 minutes, depending on the thickness of the potato pieces. The potatoes should steam to doneness with the water and then fry in the butter to make a delicious outer coat. It may be necessary to turn them once near the end of cooking, to colour them evenly.

- Remove the potatoes from the oven and set aside in a warm place. Turn up the oven to 240°C/475°F/Gas 9 or its highest temperature.
- Heat the oil in a heavy frying pan until very hot, and sear the fillet until dark brown on all sides. Transfer to the oven and roast for 40 minutes for pink, 60 minutes for well done. Remove from the oven, cover with foil and a tea cloth and allow to rest in a warm place for 10 minutes.
- Meanwhile, make the garnish. Fry the wild mushrooms in the butter and oil over a low flame for 5 minutes or so; there should be no exuding juices. Keep warm. Reheat the Red Wine Jus and check the seasoning.
- To serve, carve the beef into slices about 3cm (1¼in) thick. Set each slice on some of the pommes fondants and top with a sprig of chervil. Strew the fried mushrooms round the beef and flood the plates with the Red Wine Jus.

Wine note

This is a fantastic dish to serve with the finest your cellar has to offer as it is quite plain and allows your best claret to shine. I have some Cantermerle '73 that I'm just finishing which is perfect with this.

Winter

Venison Daube with Sloes

The left-over sloes from the autumn's sloe gin-making are perfect for this seasonal daube – their acidity cuts through the natural richness of the venison. Venison can be very lean and a little tough so this long, slow cooking is ideal to make it tender and juicy.

Serves 6
Preparation time: 30 minutes
Cooking time: 2 hours 20 minutes

1.5kg (3lb 3oz) boneless venison, cubed
4 tablespoons plain flour
3 tablespoons duck fat *or* olive oil
100ml (3½floz) port
3 tablespoons olive oil
36 baby onions, peeled
6 carrots, cut to look like the onions
500g (1lb 2oz) unsmoked bacon, cut into lardons
1 bottle red wine
bunch of fresh thyme
45g (1½oz) dried porcini
120ml (4floz) quantity of 'used' sloes from making Sloe Gin (see page 233)
black pepper

- Wash the venison to remove any blood, then dry. Dredge the pieces with the flour. Heat the duck fat in a frying pan and fry the pieces of venison until well browned. Remove to a 3 litre (5¼ pint) flameproof casserole.
- Tip away the fat from the frying pan, then deglaze with the port. Bring to the boil and pour over the venison.
- Heat the oil in the same pan and lightly brown the onions and carrots. Add to the venison. Fry the bacon until well-coloured, then move to the casserole. Deglaze the frying pan with some of the red wine and pour into the casserole.
- Add the rest of the wine to the casserole and season with black pepper. Push the thyme into the liquid. Just cover with water and bring to the boil. Reduce the heat to very low and leave to cook for 1½ hours.
- Meanwhile, soak the porcini in 240ml (8floz) boiling water for 20 minutes. Drain in a sieve set over a bowl. Filter the soaking water through kitchen paper.
- Add the sloes and the porcini with their soaking water to the casserole. Cook for a further 30 minutes. Test the venison for doneness and then serve.

Winter

Cannelloni of Hare and Thyme

You can easily make cannelloni from fresh pasta dough (see page 232), cut into rectangles measuring 12 × 15cm (5 × 6in), filled and rolled up, or you can use the ready-made dried tubes, as I have done here. Although this is an old-fashioned dish it has the fantastic rich flavours I love so much when the weather gets bleak. I have a mincer attachment for my Kenwood which is invaluable for this kind of dish.

Serves 8
Preparation time: 2 hours
Cooking time: 1 hour

6 no-cook dried cannelloni
500ml (17floz) Béchamel Sauce (see page 228)
100g (3½oz) Parmesan, freshly grated

For the sauce
100g (3½oz) pancetta, diced
6 tablespoons extra virgin olive oil
55g (2oz) onion, finely chopped
55g (2oz) carrot, finely chopped
55g (2oz) celery, finely diced
2 garlic cloves, finely chopped
800g (1¾lb) boned hare, preferably the hind legs, minced
2 sprigs of fresh thyme
1 bouquet garni
bunch of parsley
240ml (8floz) tomato passata
½ wineglass dry white wine
salt and pepper

- To make the sauce, fry the pancetta in 4 tablespoons of the olive oil in a frying pan, then add the onion, carrot, celery and garlic and cook until they are soft and golden. Transfer the pancetta and vegetables to a heavy flameproof casserole using a slotted spoon.
- Heat the remaining oil in the frying pan and fry the hare mince until well coloured. Add to the casserole together with the thyme, bouquet garni, parsley, tomato passata and wine. Bring gently to the boil. Season with salt and pepper,

then reduce the heat, cover and cook gently for 1 hour or until the hare is tender.
- Preheat the oven to 180°C/350°F/Gas 4.
- Fill the cannelloni tubes with the sauce and layer in a greased ovenproof dish. Cover with the béchamel sauce and sprinkle over the Parmesan. Bake for 1 hour.
- Serve with crusty bread and a salad

Wine note

With the effort that goes into this dish it is worth drinking a decent glass. I would favour Brunello, but a Babaresco would also be fantastic.

Winter

Sicilian Hare with Chocolate

Mexican cuisine has used chocolate in both sweet and savoury ways for hundreds of years, most notably in the classic mole *sauce for turkey, which includes three types of chillies. The dish here is not sweet – the chocolate just melts into the sauce and gives a velvety texture. The richness of the hare works really well with it. Strange but true!*

Serves 4
Preparation time: 20 minutes
Cooking time: 1 hour

1 hare, jointed and skinned
2 teaspoons paprika
6 tablespoons plain flour
100ml (3½floz) sunflower oil
12 button onions, peeled
1 teaspoon red wine vinegar
½ bottle red wine
1 litre (1¾ pints) chicken stock *or* water

1 bouquet garni
salt and pepper

To finish
75g (2½oz) raisins, plumped in 120ml (4floz) brandy
4 teaspoons liquid espresso coffee
20g (¾oz) bitter chocolate
1 teaspoon finely chopped fresh oregano

- Dredge the hare in the mixed paprika and flour. Heat the oil in a flameproof casserole and brown the joints on all sides. Remove and reserve.
- Brown the onions in the same oil; remove and reserve. Discard the oil and deglaze the casserole with the vinegar. Reduce to nothing, then add the wine. Return the hare joints and onions to the casserole, and add the stock and bouquet garni. Bring to the boil, skimming. Reduce the heat and simmer for about 45 minutes.
- Stir in the raisins and brandy, the coffee and chocolate and stir until thickened. Season to taste.
- Sprinkle with the oregano and serve from the casserole.

Winter

Kidneys with Green Peppercorns and Fresh Noodles

Without wanting to appear to have a lamb fixation, and believe me I have heard all the jokes, I think this is the perfect dish on which to end this chapter. A staple of the Edwardian breakfast table, lamb's kidneys are one of my favourite things. Whenever I do a big dinner and need to bone out large numbers of lamb saddles, I always keep the kidneys back as chef's perk if not needed for the stuffing. I think the reason most people don't like kidneys is because they usually suffer the same wretched fate as prawns – overcooking. As lean little morsels, kidneys really need to be treated with kid gloves and not overdone.

Serves 6
Preparation time: 20 minutes
Cooking time: 10 minutes

3 tablespoons sunflower oil
18 fresh lamb's kidneys, halved and the tough white interior removed
500g (1lb 2oz) fresh tagliatelle, bought or home-made (see Basic Pasta Dough, page 232)
3 tablespoons brandy
60ml (2floz) white wine
2 tablespoons green peppercorns packed in brine, drained
125ml (4½floz) crème fraîche
50g (scant 2oz) butter
2 tablespoons chopped parsley

- Heat the oil to a good temperature in a large pan and brown the kidneys all over. Remove to a warm plate.
- While the kidneys are being cooked, plunge the pasta into plenty of boiling salted water and cook for 2½–3 minutes.

- Deglaze the kidney pan with the brandy, then add the wine and reduce by half. Add the peppercorns and crème fraîche. Bubble away for 3 minutes or so to reduce.
- Drain the pasta and toss with the butter and parsley. Divide among 6 pasta plates.
- Return the kidneys and their released juices to the pan and heat through briefly in the sauce, then spoon on top of the pasta. Dress with any of the remaining sauce and consume greedily immediately.

Wine note

I quite often flame kidneys with Calvados, and then rather feel like enjoying a pint of cider with these most delicious of delicacies. Should it be mid-morning after an early start, so much the better.

Stuffed Vegetables (page 174)

Loin of Lamb with Artichokes (page 142)

Fillet of Beef with Summer Salad (page 149)

Grandmother's Handkerchiefs (page 172)

VEGETABLES

SPRING

Grandmother's Handkerchiefs

These are the most delicious pancakes, and make rather a lovely light lunch! They are called 'handkerchiefs' because of the way they are folded and then stood upright in the baking dish for the final cooking. Spinach, Parma ham and Parmesan are used for the filling, but feel free to substitute any fillings you prefer.

Makes 8
Preparation time: 1 hour
Cooking time: 16 minutes

For the pancakes
250ml (8½floz) milk
85g (3oz) plain flour
2 eggs
⅛ teaspoon salt
butter for frying

For the béchamel sauce
50g (1¾oz) butter
45g (1½oz) plain flour
500ml (17floz) milk
¼ teaspoon salt

For the filling
280g (10oz) frozen chopped spinach, thawed
3 tablespoons very finely chopped onion
15g (½oz) butter, plus more for finishing the dish
50g (1¾oz) Parma ham, chopped
140g (5oz) Parmesan, freshly grated
freshly grated nutmeg
salt and pepper

- To make the pancakes, put the milk in a bowl and add the flour gradually, mixing steadily. Add the eggs, one at a time, beating them in rapidly with a whisk. When the eggs are all incorporated, add the salt.
- Smear the bottom of a 20cm (8in) diameter crêpe pan or frying pan with a small amount of butter, then set over a medium-low heat. When the pan is hot, pour in 2 tablespoons of the pancake batter. Quickly tip the pan in several directions and rotate it so that the batter spreads out to cover the bottom

evenly. Cook until the batter sets and the base of the pancake is speckled brown. Slip a palette knife underneath it and flip the pancake over to cook the other side briefly.
- As the pancakes are cooked, stack them up on a plate. Make 8 pancakes in all. Set aside.
- Make the béchamel sauce in the usual way (see page 228). It should be rather thin.
- For the filling, drain the spinach thoroughly, squeezing it in handfuls to remove all excess water. Put the onion and butter in a small frying pan and cook over a moderate heat until the onion is soft and pale gold. Turn the onion into a bowl and add the spinach, Parma ham, all but 4 tablespoons of the Parmesan, a tiny grating of nutmeg and a pinch of salt. Add 150ml (5floz) of the béchamel. Mix until the ingredients are evenly combined, then taste and correct for salt.
- Preheat the oven to 200°C/400°F/Gas 6, and preheat the grill to high. Choose a baking dish that can accommodate all the folded pancakes in a single layer. Lightly smear the bottom of the dish with butter.
- Lay one of the pancakes on a flat surface and spread a heaped tablespoon of the filling over it. Fold loosely into four, keeping it flat, then place in the baking dish with the pointed end uppermost. Fill and fold the remaining pancakes in the same way. When they are all in the dish, spread the remaining béchamel sauce over them, making sure the sauce covers the pancakes completely. Sprinkle with the reserved Parmesan and dot butter lightly over the top.
- Bake on the top shelf of the oven for 15 minutes. Then run the dish under the hot grill for less than a minute, just long enough for a light crust to form on top. Let the pancakes settle for a few minutes, then bring to the table and serve directly from the baking dish.

Wine note

Barolo would be my choice, especially if someone else had brought it!

Spring

Stuffed Vegetables

Although there is an alarming fashion for eating pre-pubescent vegetables that have not had time to develop any flavour, there are some wonderful clean and light tastes to be savoured with small vegetables. Exactly which vegetables you use for this recipe is entirely up to you. I like courgette pieces stood up on end, red onions and baby aubergines.

Serves 6 as a starter or side dish
Preparation time: 1 hour
Cooking time: 30 minutes

18 small vegetables or pieces
1 medium onion, finely diced
2 garlic cloves, finely chopped
3 tablespoons olive oil
2 eggs, well beaten
1 tablespoon fresh thyme leaves

200g (7oz) fresh white breadcrumbs
50g (scant 2oz) butter, melted
50g (scant 2oz) Parmesan, freshly grated
salt and pepper

- If necessary, cut small vegetables in half. Hollow out the vegetables or pieces to make space for stuffing. If using aubergines, sprinkle them with salt and leave to drain for 20 minutes; rinse, drain and dry. Blanch other vegetables briefly in boiling salted water to start the softening process and to fix their colours.
- Preheat the oven to 180°C/350°F/Gas 4.
- Fry the onion and garlic gently in the oil until softened, then allow to cool slightly. Mix the egg with the thyme and breadcrumbs and season well with salt and pepper. Add the onion and mix well.
- Stuff the vegetables with the onion and thyme mixture, not packing the stuffing in too tightly. Place in a greased baking tray. Drizzle the butter over the vegetables and sprinkle with the cheese. Bake for about 30 minutes or until the smell of the vegetables starts to waft around you and your gastric juices start to flow. Serve hot or warm with a little extra oil and bread.

Spring

Thai Yellow Bean Cakes with Tamarind Dip

Without being desperately sandal-wearing, these are delicious and vegetarian. The tamarind sauce really gives these morsels a lift. They can be served as part of a Thai meal or as a starter, and also make a great addition to a buffet.

Makes 16–20
Preparation time: 45 minutes
Cooking time: 10 minutes

For the bean cakes
115g (4oz) dried *moong dal* (hulled and split mung beans), soaked in water for 30 minutes and drained
1 tablespoon rice flour
1 teaspoon salt
½ teaspoon white pepper
1 teaspoon sugar
1 teaspoon ground cumin
oil for deep-frying

For the tamarind dip
3 large fresh red chillies, chopped
1 large garlic clove, chopped
2 shallots, finely chopped
3 tablespoons tamarind water (see page 231)
1 tablespoon sugar
pinch of salt

- In a food processor, blend the drained *moong dal* to form a paste. Add the rice flour, salt, pepper, sugar and cumin, mixing well. Pluck small pieces of the paste and form into balls the size of a walnut. Do not mould too tightly. Set aside.
- To make the dip, pound the chillies, garlic and shallots together in a mortar. When well pounded, stir in the tamarind water, sugar and salt and mix well together. Turn into a small bowl.
- Deep-fry the balls in oil heated to 190°C/375°F until golden brown all over. Drain on kitchen paper and serve with the tamarind dip.

Spring

Courgette, Pea and Mint Pie

This pie actually tastes better when warm as opposed to hot, and it sets when a little colder. Do make sure that there is no moisture likely to leak from the courgettes.

Serves 10 as a main dish
Preparation time: 55 minutes
Cooking time: 1½ hours

340g (12oz) ready-rolled puff pastry
1 large onion, finely chopped
2 garlic cloves, finely chopped
3 tablespoons olive oil
6 large, firm courgettles, halved lengthways and cut into 5mm (¼in) slices
6 eggs, lightly beaten
250g (9oz) fresh ricotta
30g (1oz) fresh mint leaves, shredded
280g (10oz) thawed frozen peas or blanched fresh peas
150g (5½oz) Parmesan, freshly grated
salt and pepper

- Preheat the oven to 180°C/350°F/Gas 4.
- Line a greased loose-bottomed 20cm (8in) round tin with the pastry, reserving a circle to fit the top.
- Fry the onion and the garlic in the oil until softened. Add the courgettes and continue to cook, turning constantly to evaporate any excess liquid. On a low heat, this could take 10 minutes. Add a little more oil if necessary.
- Reserve a teaspoon of the beaten egg and mix the remainder with the ricotta. Season with salt and pepper. Fold in the mint, then add the peas and the contents of the frying pan and mix very well.
- Tip the mixture into the pastry-lined tin and cover with the circle of pastry. Make a small hole in the top and crimp around the edge to seal. Glaze the top with the reserved egg.
- Bake for about 1½ hours. To check for doneness, insert a skewer into the middle of the pie and leave for 20 seconds; it should come out hot.

Spring

Roman Fried Artichokes

Globe artichokes are a favourite of the Romans and were traditionally eaten in the ghetto there. Although a little time-consuming to prepare, fresh artichokes are a treat.

Serves 4 as a side dish
Preparation time: 35 minutes
Cooking time: 5 minutes

4 large globe artichokes
½ lemon
1 lemon, cut into pieces

4 tablespoons plain flour
sunflower oil for deep-frying
salt

- In preparing any artichoke, it is essential to discard all the tough, inedible leaves. Begin by bending back the outer leaves, pulling them down towards the base of the artichoke and snapping them off just before you reach the base. Do not take off the paler bottom end of the leaf because at that point it is tender and quite edible. Slice at least 2.5 cm (1in) off the top of that central cone to eliminate all the tough green part. Remove the chokes. Take the half lemon and rub over the cut surfaces of the artichoke, squeezing juice over them to keep them from discolouring. Don't cut off the stalk, which for this dish must remain attached.
- Turn the artichoke upside down, and you will notice that the bottom of the stalk consists of a whitish core surrounded by a layer of green. The green part is tough, so pare the stalk all the way to the base of the artichoke, being careful not to detach it. Rub all the exposed cut surfaces with lemon juice.
- Cook the artichokes in simmering salted water, with the cut up lemon in it, for 12 minutes or until tender. Remove from the water and dry quite well. Squash the round part on a work surface so the remaining leaves are splayed out.
- Work a little water into the flour to make a simple batter with the consistency of double cream.
- Heat a deep pan of sunflower oil to 190°C/375°F (see page 100). Dip the artichokes in the batter and deep-fry until golden. Drain on kitchen paper, sprinkle with salt, serve.

Summer

Stuffed Courgette Flowers

Another Roman treat, courgette flowers make the most delicate of toppings for a pizza bianca *and are often stuffed with ricotta-based fillings and fried as here. The trick is to make them tasty but ever so light.*

Makes 8 as a starter
Preparation time: 30 minutes
Cooking time: 8 minutes

1 medium onion, finely chopped
2 garlic cloves, finely chopped
30g (1oz) butter
3 anchovy fillets, preferably packed in brine, from the deli counter, rather than canned (optional)
250g (9oz) ricotta
15g (½oz) fresh basil leaves, finely shredded

8 courgette flowers
sunflower oil for deep-frying

For the batter
2 eggs
300ml (10floz) whole milk
170g (6oz) plain flour
1 teaspoon baking powder
salt and black pepper

- First make the batter. Beat the eggs with a pinch of salt and liberal amounts of pepper, then work in the milk. Sift in the flour and baking powder and mix until smooth. Allow to rest for 30 minutes before using.
- To make the stuffing, gently sauté the onion and garlic in the butter to soften but not colour. If using the anchovy fillets, add to the pan and cook, breaking them up with a wooden spoon so they dissolve into the butter and onions.
- Beat the ricotta until fluffy and season with black pepper (the anchovies are salty, so only add salt if not using anchovies). Stir into the onion mixture together with the basil.
- Divide the filling mixture into 8 portions and carefully stuff the courgette flowers. Dip into the batter, shake off excess and deep-fry in oil heated to 190°C/375°F or until a day-old cube of bread browns in 1 minute, for about 4 minutes or until browned. Drain well on kitchen paper and eat immediately.

Summer

White Radish Cake with Bean Sprouts and Spring Onions

Strict Buddhists will not eat animal flesh and so have developed vegetarian food to an art. This white radish cake is vegan in fact, and I refer to it as Buddhist chicken because it can be stir-fried or curried in the same way as poultry. It does sound like a really strange dish, but is delicious and very unusual. Any flavours you can think of can be introduced into the radish mixture before it is cooked, such as garlic, mushrooms or fresh coriander.

Serves 3 as a main dish or 6 as part of a Chinese meal
Preparation time: 1 hour
Cooking time: 5 minutes

1 white radish (also called mooli or daikon), about 450g (1lb)
85g (3oz) rice flour
30g (1oz) plain flour
3 tablespoons sunflower oil
2 garlic cloves, finely crushed
1 egg
2 tablespoons light soy sauce
1 tablespoon dark soy sauce
½ teaspoon sugar
30g (1oz) fresh bean sprouts, rinsed and drained
3 spring onions, cut into 2.5cm (1in) slivers
white pepper

- Peel the radish and cut into small cubes. Using a food processor or blender, mash the radish as finely as possible. This will have to be done in two batches. Mix the radish thoroughly with the rice and plain flours. Turn the mixture into a shallow tin or heatproof dish about 20cm (8in) square; it should make a layer about 2cm (¾in) thick.
- Heat up a steamer and steam the radish cake for about 30 minutes from the time the water starts boiling. If you are using a thicker dish you will have to

steam it for a little longer. When an inserted knife comes out clean, remove from the heat and allow to cool and dry out completely. It will set more solidly as it cools.
- Cut the radish cake into squares about 2.5 × 2.5cm (1 × 1in).
- Heat half the oil in a wok, add the radish cake squares and fry, turning constantly, until they are browned on all sides. Remove from the wok and set aside.
- Add the rest of the oil to the wok and heat. Add the garlic and fry until golden brown. Break in the egg, stir to mix with the garlic and cook for a few seconds until the egg starts to set. Add the fried radish cake squares and mix with the egg. Quickly add both the soy sauces, the sugar, bean sprouts and spring onions. Season with pepper. Mix quickly but thoroughly, then turn on to a serving dish.

Summer

Red Onion, Feta and Pine Nut Pizza

If you make this in the traditional boat shape, it is redolent of a felucca, *a boat that is seen on the Nile. When I stayed at the old Cataract Hotel, scene of* Murder on the Nile, *they served a similar flat bread with onions. The word for bread in Arabic is the same as that for life, and whether leavened or not this staple sustains a third of the world.*

Serves 4 as a light dish
Preparation time: 1 hour 20 minutes
Cooking time: 10 minutes

50g (1lb) red onions, finely sliced
5–6 tablespoons olive oil
1 tablespoon pine nuts
1 quantity of risen Focaccia dough (see page 233)

200g (7oz) feta cheese, crumbled
16 black olives, stoned and chopped
freshly grated nutmeg
salt and pepper

- Preheat the oven to 240°C/475°F/Gas 9 or its highest setting.
- Soften the onions in a little of the olive oil until translucent, then reserve.
- Toast the pine nuts in a dry pan over a low heat for about 2 minutes or until golden, stirring frequently.
- Divide the dough into quarters and roll out each into a long oval about 30 x 20cm (12 x 8in). Distribute the onions, feta, olives and pine nuts over them, leaving a clear rim of about 4cm (1½in). Pull the sides up and over towards the middle. Season with grated nutmeg, salt and pepper. Bake for 10 minutes.

Summer

Pattypan Squash Braised with Rosemary and White Wine

I have to confess that pretty as these vegetables are, and much as I use them, they've never really grown on me because they're usually picked before much flavour has developed. Also, they tend to be watery. This is the only way I've found to cook pattypan squash (also called custard marrow) so they retain their freshness and colour and have a decent flavour. The same technique can be applied to courgette pieces.

Serves 6 as a side dish
Preparation time: 30 minutes
Cooking time: 16 minutes

500g (1lb 2oz) pattypan squash
60ml (2floz) olive oil
2 garlic cloves, crushed and well chopped
120ml (4floz) white wine
2 sprigs of fresh rosemary, 10cm (4in) long, needles only
salt and pepper

- Top, tail and quarter the squashes. Sprinkle with 2 tablespoons salt and allow to drain for 20 minutes as you would with aubergines. Rinse and dry.
- Heat a sauté pan and add the olive oil. When the oil is about to smoke, add the squash pieces and sauté for 5 minutes, stirring constantly, until they have coloured.
- Add the garlic and stir to mix, then add the wine and rosemary needles. Season well with salt and pepper. Cover with a lid, reduce the heat to the lowest possible heat and continue to cook for 10 minutes. The liquid that is produced will rise as steam, then run back into the pan and continue the steaming process as long as the heat is not too high. Serve hot.

SUMMER

French Bean Salad with Tarator Sauce

This is a southern French dish which sounds rather odd but is delicious. I made it on Light Lunch *before snogging both of the girls, Mel and Sue. Good thing we'd not eaten first as the garlic is quite pungent. Walnuts are traditional, but I'm allergic to them so I use pecans. In the same way I replace peanuts with cashews, which may help some of you.*

Serves 6 as a side dish
Preparation time: 10 minutes

450g (1lb) fine French beans
115g (4oz) walnut or pecan pieces
55g (2oz) fresh white breadcrumbs
3 garlic cloves, peeled

2 tablespoons lemon juice
150ml (5floz) olive oil
salt and pepper

- Blanch the beans in rapidly boiling salted water for 4 minutes, then refresh in cold water and drain.
- Put the nuts, breadcrumbs, garlic and lemon juice into a food processor. Season with salt and pepper and process to a paste. Then, with the machine running, add the olive oil in a thin stream to make a smooth purée.
- Spoon the sauce over the beans and toss to coat. If coated whilst hot they will absorb more flavour.

Autumn

Mushroom Filo Pie

This is a really rich and delicious accompaniment for simply roasted meat or can be served as a vegetarian main course. The use of the filo pastry makes life very easy indeed. Flat field mushrooms give the best-flavoured result.

Serves 4 as a main dish or 6 as a side dish
Preparation time: 45 minutes
Cooking time: 30 minutes

500g (1lb 2oz) onions, finely diced
4 garlic cloves, finely chopped
4 tablespoons olive oil
1.5kg (3lb 3oz) mixed mushrooms, sliced
a 400g (14oz) can chick peas, drained and rinsed
1 tablespoon fresh thyme leaves
600ml (1 pint) double cream
25g (scant 1oz) butter, melted
6 sheets filo pastry
2 tablespoons sesame seeds
salt and pepper

- Fry the onions and garlic in the oil to soften but not to colour. Add the mushrooms and continue to cook. The mushrooms will start to collapse and release a lot of moisture; seasoning early on encourages this. Continue cooking until all the liquid has evaporated. Stir in the chick peas and thyme. Add the cream and bubble away gently until the cream has all but gone and you have a delicious mass of richly flavoured mushrooms.
- Transfer to a greased ovenproof casserole or similar (I use one that is 32cm/13in long and 5cm/2in deep).
- Preheat the oven to 180°C/350°F/Gas 4.
- Butter and layer 3 of the sheets of filo, then cover the top of the pie with these. Butter the remaining sheets and scrunch up like old brown paper. Lay these over the top so you have an interesting texture. Sprinkle with the sesame seeds.
- Bake for 30 minutes or until browned and delicious. Serve hot.

Autumn

Tomato and Basil Tart

This is really so easy and makes a nice change from the usual tarte fine *made with flaky pastry. It's a great opportunity to use the fantastic oil you brought back from your holidays, or were given for Christmas, as the heat of the fresh tart will release the most wonderful aromas from the oil. Of course, unless the tomatoes are good quality, the dish will be dull.*

Serves 4–6 as a starter
Preparation time: 40 minutes
Cooking time: 15 minutes

500g (1lb 2oz) best quality tomatoes
2 tablespoons best olive oil
15g (½oz) fresh basil leaves

For the pastry
55g (generous 2oz) butter, duck fat *or*
olive oil
125g (4 ½oz) plain flour
125g (4 ½oz) leftover mashed potatoes
sea salt and pepper

- Slice the tomatoes, sprinkle with sea salt and add a little of the olive oil. Leave to marinate, which will draw out a little of the excess moisture and will season them well.
- Meanwhile, make the pastry. Rub the fat into the flour and mix in the mashed potato. Add just enough water to make a smooth dough. Allow it to rest for 15 minutes.
- Preheat the oven to 180°C/350°F/Gas 4.
- Lightly flour a non-stick 30cm (12in) square baking tray. Roll out the pastry to fit and use to line the tray. Prick all over with a fork, then cover with foil and weight down with baking beans. Bake for 10 minutes.
- Remove from the oven and take off the foil and beans. Drain the tomato slices and arrange over the pastry. Season with pepper
- Increase the oven temperature to 200°C/400°F/Gas 6 and bake the tart for 15 minutes. Drizzle with the remaining olive oil and strew the basil leaves over the top. Cut into pieces at table.

Autumn

Vegetable Couscous

Couscous, unlike bulghur wheat, with which it is often confused, is made from durum wheat and consequently is very bland. It needs lots of tender loving care to make it taste of something. Harissa can be bought in most supermarkets or halal butchers. The Moroccan Bread Pinwheels on page 11 would be an ideal first course before this for a vegetarian meal with a twist.

Serves 4 as a main dish
Preparation time: 20 minutes plus 30 minutes resting
Cooking time: 1 hour

2 large courgettes, cut into 3cm (1¼in) chunks
2 medium aubergines, cut into 3cm (1¼in) chunks
12 medium tomatoes, halved
2 large red peppers, quartered lengthways
4 large garlic cloves, crushed
1 large onion, thinly sliced
4 tablespoons olive oil
sprigs of fresh coriander to garnish (optional)

For the couscous
250g (9oz) couscous
55g (2oz) butter

For the sauce
4 tablespoons olive oil
1 medium onion, finely chopped
510ml (18floz) tomato passata
2 teaspoons harissa paste
salt and pepper

- Put the courgettes and aubergines into a colander and sprinkle with 2 tablespoons of salt. Toss them around, then leave them for 30 minutes. This will break down the flesh so that the vegetables don't soak up too much oil when they are cooked.
- Preheat the oven to 200°C/400°F/Gas 6.
- Rinse the aubergines and courgettes, dry them and put them in a large roasting tin with the tomatoes, peppers, crushed garlic and onion. Drizzle with the olive oil and grind some black pepper over everything. Bake for about 35 minutes, turning occasionally.

- Put the couscous in a deep ovenproof pot and pour over just enough cold water to cover. Leave for 5 minutes, by which time the couscous will have soaked up the water. Fluff up the grains with a fork, dot with the butter and cover with foil. Bake in the oven with the vegetables for the remainder of their cooking time (about 30 minutes).
- Meanwhile, make the spicy tomato sauce. Heat the olive oil in a saucepan, add the onion and cook for 5 minutes over a moderate heat until soft. Add the tomato passata and the harissa paste. Grind in some salt and black pepper, then leave to simmer gently for 15 minutes or until thick and soupy.
- Remove the foil from the couscous and fluff up the grains with a fork. Put a pile of the couscous on each plate and top with some of the warm vegetables. Spoon over the spicy tomato sauce, adding a sprig of coriander to garnish if you wish.

Wine note

The richness of the vegetable flavours suggests the excellent Lebanese red made by Gaston Hochar at Chateau Musar.

Autumn

Swiss Chard Fritters

When I was a kid my father used to grow Swiss chard, although we knew it as silver beet. A large, leafy vegetable, it has very dark, glossy leaves and white ribs like a cardoon. It is a favourite in the north of Italy and, although available here, it seems to be only Italy and New Zealand that hold it dear. It is so full of iron it's a wonder it doesn't rust!

Makes 12
Preparation time: 40 minutes
Cooking time: 12 minutes

12 leaves Swiss chard
1 medium onion, finely diced
2 garlic cloves, finely chopped
2 tablespoons olive oil
250g (9oz) ricotta
150g (5½oz) Parmesan, freshly grated
200g (7oz) fresh white breadcrumbs
15g (½oz) fresh sage leaves, finely sliced
4 eggs, lightly beaten
oil for deep-frying
salt and pepper
Fresh Tomato Sauce (see page 228) to serve

- Separate the green leafy part from the stalks of the chard. Shred the leafy part, then steam until tender and wilted; drain well, squeezing out excess moisture. Reserve in a mixing bowl. Trim the white stalks so each gives two pieces 8cm (3¼in) long. Blanch in boiling salted water for 1 minute, then drain. Set aside.
- Fry the onion and garlic in the oil until soft but not coloured. Tip into the bowl with the leafy parts of the chard and add the ricotta and Parmesan. Season well and mix together.
- Put the pieces of chard stalk together in pairs, pairing the thicker part of one stalk with the thicker part of another. Use the ricotta mixture to hold each pair of chard stalks together and neaten, removing any excess mixture. Mix the breadcrumbs with the sage. Dip the chard 'sandwiches' in the beaten egg, then coat with the crumb mixture.
- Deep-fry in oil heated to 190°C/375°F (see page 100) until well browned all over. Drain on kitchen paper and serve with fresh tomato sauce.

Autumn

Lentil Moussaka

Lentils from Puy in France are glossy olive-green in colour and very small compared to the brown or green versions. Unlike their larger cousins they have plenty of flavour and no muddy aftertaste. They cook in unsalted water in 15 minutes and need no presoaking. Although lentils have a negative, sandal-wearing image, they offer great flavour and are a good source of protein for vegetarians as well as for those cutting back on cholesterol. This is a very healthy version of moussaka, but if you prefer the aubergines could be fried rather than grilled and twice the quantity of béchamel sauce could be made and layered through the dish.

Serves 8 as a light lunch or 12 as a side dish
Preparation time: 1 hour
Cooking time: 1 hour

800g (1¾lb) long aubergines, cut lengthways into 5mm (¼in) slices
250g (9oz) Puy lentils
1kg (2¼lb) fresh tomatoes
300g (10½oz) onions, finely chopped
3 garlic cloves, chopped
2 tablespoons extra virgin olive oil
15g (½oz) fresh basil leaves
50g (scant 2oz) Parmesan, freshly grated

For the béchamel sauce
30g (1oz) butter
2 tablespoons plain flour
500ml (17floz) whole milk
¼ nutmeg, freshly grated
salt and black pepper

- Sprinkle the aubergine slices with salt and leave to drain for 30 minutes
- Meanwhile, cook the lentils in plenty of unsalted water for 15 minutes. Drain and rinse, then leave to drain fully.
- Blend the tomatoes to a pulp (there is no need to peel or seed them). Fry the onions and garlic in the oil until soft and translucent. Add the tomatoes, 1 teaspoon salt and a generous amount of black pepper. Stir through the lentils. Shred the basil and stir in.
- Drain, rinse and dry the aubergine slices. Grill on a hot ridged cast-iron grill pan until well marked on both sides and soft. Reserve.

- Preheat the oven to 180°C/350°F/Gas 4. Grease an ovenproof dish – I use one that is 32 × 23cm (13 × 9in) and 5cm (2in) deep. The larger the surface area, the larger the amount of crispy crust!
- Make the béchamel sauce (see page 228).
- Spread one-third of the lentil mixture on the bottom of the buttered dish and arrange a third of the aubergine slices over to cover the lentils. Repeat the layers twice, finishing with aubergine slices. Spread the béchamel sauce over the surface and sprinkle with the Parmesan.
- Bake for 1 hour or until browned and bubbling. Serve hot or warm.

Wine note

A robust red, such as Berry Brothers good ordinary claret, would be ideal. Alternatively, with the '70s revival, a raffia-covered Chianti flask – for later conversion into a lamp base – might be more thematic!

Winter

Plantain and Spinach Curry

The plantain is a relation of the banana but is much starchier and has a very pleasant flavour. It is a staple in Caribbean and African communities. I buy plantains in Portobello market for next to nothing. This curry is a real treat and must be oozing with vitamins.

Serves 6 as a side dish or part of a larger meal
Preparation time: 10 minutes
Cooking time: 15 minutes

1 onion, thinly sliced
3 garlic cloves, thinly sliced
a 2cm (¾in) piece of fresh ginger, peeled and thinly sliced
1 tablespoon sunflower oil
1 teaspoon tumeric
1 teaspoon black mustard seeds
2 large plantains, peeled and cut into 2cm (¾in) chunks
360ml (12floz) coconut milk
200g (7oz) spinach leaves

- Fry the onion, garlic and ginger in the oil until softened. Add the turmeric and mustard seeds and continue frying until the seeds pop, stirring constantly.
- Add the plantains and stir to coat in the mixture. Add the coconut milk and spinach. Cover and cook on a low heat for about 8 minutes, stirring occasionally.

Winter

Onion Bhajias with Coriander Chutney

Chick pea flour has a slightly gritty texture and a delicious flavour, and provides protein to large numbers of vegetarians in India.

Makes about 12
Preparation time: 20 minutes
Cooking time: 12 minutes

For the bhajias
225g (8oz) chick pea flour
2 teaspoons cumin seeds
½ teaspoon dried chilli flakes
2 teaspoons chopped fresh coriander
1 teaspoon salt
½ teaspoon bicarbonate of soda
2 medium onions, very thinly sliced
oil for deep-frying

For the chutney
50g (scant 2oz) toasted cashews, very finely chopped
100g (3½oz) fresh coriander leaves, finely chopped
3 fresh green chillies, seeded and finely chopped (to taste)
a thumbnail-sized piece of fresh ginger, peeled and finely chopped
pinch of salt
pinch of sugar
1 tablespoon lemon or lime juice
1 teaspoon sunflower oil

- Mix together all the ingredients for the bhajias, except the onions, and add about 100ml (3½floz) of warm water to form a thickish batter. The consistency should be like lightly whipped cream. Stir in the onions. Leave to rest for 5 minutes to allow the bicarbonate of soda to work.
- Meanwhile, mix all the chutney ingredients together in a bowl.
- Fry tablespoonfuls of the onion mixture in oil heated to 190°C/375°F (see page 100) for about 3 minutes or until browned all over (don't make them too large). Drain on kitchen paper and serve as soon as possible, with the chutney.

Winter

Sweetcorn Fritters and Salsa

As a child, sweetcorn fritters were a staple of Saturday lunches with 'tommy K' (tomato ketchup). This is a slightly more sophisticated version that takes the sweetcorn from New Zealand to Mexico and gives it a chilli kick. These are great at a barbecue or as an accompaniment to simply grilled steaks or fried chicken.

Serves 4–6 as a light lunch
Preparation time: 20 minutes
Cooking time: 15 minutes

For the fritters
2 eggs
2 tablespoons caster sugar
1 teaspoon salt
240ml (8floz) milk
450g (1lb) plain flour
2 teaspoons baking powder
kernels from 2 corn-on-the-cob
4 tablespoons finely chopped fresh coriander
sunflower oil for frying

For the salsa
1 red pepper
1 yellow pepper
1 beef tomato
1 fresh red chilli
15g (½oz) fresh coriander, finely chopped
juice of 2 limes
100ml (3½floz) olive oil

- To make the salsa, finely chop the peppers, tomato and chilli and combine with the coriander, lime juice and olive oil. Season. Leave for up to 30 minutes to soften, but no longer or the salsa will go slushy. (To prepare in advance, finely chop the vegetables and mix together, but do not dress with the lime juice and oil until ready to serve.)
- Beat the eggs with the sugar and salt and add a little of the milk. Stir in the flour and baking powder, then make into a stiffish batter with the rest of the milk. Add the sweetcorn kernels and coriander and stir through the batter.

- Heat a pan of oil for shallow-frying. Drop spoonfuls of the batter into the hot oil in 5–7.5cm (2–3in) blobs and fry until golden brown on both sides. Drain on kitchen paper and keep warm until all the fritters are fried, then serve, with the salsa.

> **Wine note**
>
> A Margarita is the first drink that comes to mind, or hand.

Winter

Yellow Curry of Aubergines

In the depths of winter, Asian food – with all its flavours redolent of the sun – always comes to mind. The delight of this dish is being able to use the vast variety of aubergines we can now get, from the tiny pea aubergines, which just need blanching, to the original round white ones which gave this vegetable its other name, 'eggplant' (when the first Portuguese explorers found it in India, it had not been bred into the purple varieties we know today). The Thais have long, green aubergines and the Indians have wonderful yellow ones. It's really worth searching out a good variety for the eye-appeal they give this dish.

Serves 4 as part of a larger meal
Preparation time: 15 minutes
Cooking time: 15 minutes

1kg (2¼lb) mixed aubergines
2 tablespoons yellow curry paste
2 tablespoons sunflower oil
400ml (14floz) coconut milk

juice of 2 limes
12 fresh lime leaves, shredded
15g (½oz) fresh coriander leaves
salt

- Cut the aubergines into appropriate shapes – diamonds, halves or quarters. The easiest way to cut diamonds from the large purple variety is to top and tail the fruits and then cut across into about 8 segments. Cut the outer 2cm (¾in) away from the spongy core (discard the core) and then cut each of the strips at an angle into diamond shapes. Sprinkle all the aubergines with salt and leave to drain in a colander for 20 minutes. Rinse, drain and dry.
- Fry the curry paste in the oil in a saucepan. When the aroma starts to develop add the coconut milk and bring to the boil. Add the aubergines and simmer for 7–8 minutes.
- When ready to serve, stir in the lime juice and shredded lime leaves to sharpen the taste, then add the coriander. Serve with rice.

WINTER

Root Vegetable Gratin

This is a version of the classic gratin dauphinoise of 'la belle France'. It is ideal with roast lamb or with pork. The tarragon isn't essential, although it does give a wonderful, almost smoky flavour. There is no garlic in this recipe, but feel free to add it. I once served this with a fillet of beef to a friend who was in London with his wife for the International Gold Council. It turned out to be Valerie's 40th birthday, so I will always think of this as a celebration dish. A delicious version can be made with just turnips, tarragon and prunes.

Serves 8 as a side dish
Preparation time: 20 minutes
Cooking time: 1½ hours

500g (1lb 2oz) sweet potatoes
500g (1lb 2oz) swede
500g (1lb 2oz) celeriac
500g (1lb 2oz) parsnips

550ml (18½floz) double cream
15g (½oz) fresh tarragon leaves
salt and pepper

- Preheat the oven to 180°C/350°F/Gas 4.
- Peel the vegetables and cut into 5mm (¼in) slices, keeping each vegetable separate. Mix each with a quarter of the cream and the tarragon and season with salt and pepper.
- Layer the vegetables in an ovenproof dish, finishing with the sweet potato. Make the top quite neat
- Bake for 1½ hours. To check for doneness, test with a small knife. Leftovers, should there be any, are wonderful puréed and reheated the next day.

Wine note

It depends on the rest of the meal, but the sweetness is great with an old, smoky claret.

PUDDINGS

Spring

Lime Tart with Passion Fruit Sauce

Sour lemon tart is a staple of French bistros and 1970s dinner parties. With a nod to Saint Delia, the lemon is replaced here by the citrus of the 1990s, lime. Fresh lime juice gives a cleaner tang, although bottled is much cheaper. The tropical theme is carried through with the passion fruit. The passion flower, which has nothing to do with lust, was used by South American missionaries to teach Christ's passion. The flower has layers of petals, sepals and stigma that are numbered to correspond to the Holy Trinity and the Apostles, and has a band of thorn-like structures representing Christ's crown of thorns. A great pudding for Lent!

Serves 10
Preparation time: 30 minutes plus 3 hours resting
Cooking time: 40 minutes

For the pastry
250g (9oz) plain flour
125g (4½oz) butter
15g (½oz) caster sugar
½ teaspoon salt
1 egg

For the filling
1 tablespoon arrowroot
300ml (10floz) fresh or bottled lime juice (not cordial)

4 eggs, beaten
150g (5½oz) sugar
100g (3½oz) butter, chilled and diced
icing sugar to finish (optional)

For the passion fruit sauce
10 passion fruit
150g (5½oz) caster sugar
knob of butter (optional)

- First make the pastry. Put the flour, butter, sugar and salt in a food processor and process until they form a crumb-like mixture. Add the egg and process for a further 30 seconds. Add a splash of water and process for 30 seconds. If the mixture does not form a ball in the food processor, add another splash of water

and process for a further 30 seconds. Repeat until a homogeneous dough forms.
- Remove the dough from the processor and roll out on a floured surface to a thickness of 4mm (scant ¼in). Use to line a 24cm (9½in) loose-based tart tin. Pierce the bottom with a fork several times, then chill for at least 3 hours to allow the gluten in the flour to relax.
- Preheat the oven to 180°C/350°F/Gas 4.
- Line the pastry case with foil and weight down with baking beans. Bake blind for 15 minutes, then remove the foil and beans and continue baking until the pastry just crisps but doesn't colour. Set aside. Leave the oven on.
- Mix the arrowroot with a little of the lime juice, then stir in the rest. Pour into a saucepan and add the eggs and sugar. Beat well to combine. Cook over a very low heat until the mixture starts to thicken, stirring constantly. Beat in the butter. Set aside to cool for a bit.
- Fill the pastry case with the lime mixture. Bake for 20 minutes. Do not overcook or the filling will curdle and will not set. Allow to go cold
- To make the sauce, cut the passion fruit in half and scoop the pulp into a saucepan. Add the sugar and simmer for 5 minutes. Put into a food processor fitted with the plastic blade and process for 1 minute to dislodge the seeds from the pulp. Press through a sieve. Add a knob of butter to the sauce if a scum forms (this should dissolve any impurities). Chill.
- To serve, dust the tart with icing sugar or leave plain, and serve with the sauce.

Spring

Rhubarb and Almond Cream Tart

Rhubarb is the most wonderful of vegetables. Although deeply astringent it has a fantastic depth of flavour. It is so named because it was brought over the Rhu (the Volga) by the Barbarians (they can't have been that bad then, to bring a great pudding with them when they rampaged!). The filling puffs up around the rhubarb as it cooks, like the apple and prune cake on page 215.

Serves 10
Preparation time: 30 minutes plus 3 hours resting
Cooking time: 1¼ hours

For the pastry
250g (9oz) plain flour
125g (4½oz) butter
scant 1 tablespoon caster sugar
scant 1 teaspoon salt
1 egg

For the filling
200g (7oz) caster sugar
450g (1lb) rhubarb, cut into 2.5cm (1in) pieces

For the almond cream
250g (9oz) unsalted butter
250g (9oz) icing sugar
250g (9oz) ground almonds
50g (scant 2oz) plain flour
3 eggs
2 tablespoons Maraschino liqueur
icing sugar to dust

- First make the pastry. Put the flour, butter, sugar and salt in a food processor and process until they form a crumb-like mixture. Add the egg and process for a further 30 seconds. Add a splash of water and process for 30 seconds. If the mixture does not form a ball in the food processor, add another splash of water and process for a further 30 seconds. Repeat until a homogeneous dough forms.
- Remove the dough from the processor and roll out on a floured surface to a thickness of 4mm (scant ¼in). Use to line a 21cm (8½in) loose-based tart tin.

Pierce the bottom with a fork several times, then chill for at least 3 hours to allow the gluten in the flour to relax.
- Preheat the oven to 180°C/350°F/Gas 4.
- Line the pastry case with foil and weight down with baking beans. Bake blind for 15 minutes, then remove the foil and beans and continue baking until the pastry just crisps but doesn't colour.
- Meanwhile, combine the sugar and 400ml (14floz) water in a saucepan. Bring to a simmer, stirring to dissolve the sugar. Add the rhubarb and poach for 1 minute. Drain well and set aside.
- To make the almond cream, beat the butter until fluffy. Mix the sugar and almonds together and mix into the butter, then add the flour. Beat in the eggs, one at a time, and then add the Maraschino.
- Spread the almond cream into the pastry case and arrange the poached rhubarb over the cream. Bake for about 45 minutes or until the cream has set. Cool before serving, dusted with icing sugar.

Wine note

With the gentle richness of this pudding, a sweet Coteaux du Layon from the Loire would be perfect.

SPRING

24 Carat Brûlée

Crème brûlée has made a huge return as a vastly trendy pudding, but has not been left to rest on its laurels – every restaurant in the land now has a version. A favourite of mine is a tarragon flavouring, which is surprisingly good. The crunchy topping reminds me of what we called hokey-pokey ice-cream in New Zealand. The story goes that around the turn of the century, ice-cream sellers would use barrows in cities to move their wares and, being Italian, would cry out 'ho che poco' ('it costs so little'), hence our 'hokey-pokey'.

Serves 6
Preparation time: 20 minutes plus setting time
Cooking time: 5 minutes

600ml (1 pint) double cream
½ teaspoon saffron threads
4 egg yolks, lightly beaten
1 tablespoon chopped stem ginger
1 tablespoon syrup from the stem ginger
about 100g (3½oz) caster sugar

- Put the cream and saffron into a saucepan and bring almost to the boil. Pour over the egg yolks, add the ginger and syrup and stir to mix. Return to the pan and cook gently, stirring constantly, until the custard is thick enough to 'coat' the back of the spoon.
- Pour the custard into 6 ramekins and leave to go cold, then chill well until set.
- Sprinkle each custard with 1 teaspoon of caster sugar. Melt the sugar with a blowtorch or under a hot grill. Repeat this two or three times to build up a good layer of hard caramel. Take care not to overheat the sugar or the heat will penetrate the custard and melt it. Return to the fridge to harden the caramel. (Don't leave the pudding in the fridge longer than 2–3 hours before serving.)
- Alternatively, you can use the cheat's version: melt the sugar and cook until it turns golden brown, then pour this molten caramel on to the custards. Allow to set before serving.

Clockwise from top right: Deep Raspberry Tart (page 209); Dark and White Chocolate Tart (page 226); Lime Tart (page 198)

Poached Pear with Lime
Caramel Sauce (page 217)

Steamed Squash with Coconut and Ginger Custard (page 203)

Cooking for friends should be fun!

SPRING

Steamed Squash with Coconut and Ginger Custard

This most unusual dessert is an adaptation of a traditional Thai pudding. The Thais have developed a variety of squash, with a wonderful mottled skin, just for making this pudding; if you cannot find it, a kabocha squash will do very well as a substitute. The addition of ginger and saffron make the pudding particularly fragrant.

Serves 8
Preparation time: 20 minutes
Cooking time: 1 hour

1 squash such as kabocha, about 1kg (2¼lb)
130ml (4¼floz) double cream
100ml (3½floz) coconut milk from a well-shaken can
125g (4½oz) palm sugar *or* caster sugar
pinch of saffron
1 ball stem ginger, drained and finely chopped
4 eggs

- Cut a hole in the top of the squash; lift off and reserve this lid. Scrape out the seeds and fibres from the centre of the squash to make a hollow.
- Combine the double cream, coconut cream, sugar and saffron in a saucepan and bring almost to the boil, stirring to dissolve the sugar. Remove from the heat and stir in the ginger.
- Lightly beat the eggs in a bowl. Pour in the cream mixture and mix thoroughly. Pour into the squash. (The custard should not completely fill the squash as the custard will expand during cooking.) Replace the lid.
- Steam the squash for 1 hour. Allow to cool and then chill.
- Serve cold, cut into wedges. (Everything is edible except the skin of the squash.)

Spring

Wicked Chocolate Brownies

Gooey and chocolatey, these really are yummy! They're good for a lunchbox or as an easy pudding with best-quality vanilla ice-cream. Even without a sweet tooth I can force a few of these down, especially with coffee when the sugar low hits mid-afternoon. To be really posh, they can be cut into circles and served with clotted cream.

Makes about 12 squares
Preparation time: 20 minutes
Cooking time: 40 minutes

145g (generous 5oz) butter, at room temperature
200g (7oz) caster sugar
2 eggs

115g (4oz) plain flour
85g (3oz) cocoa powder
55g (2oz) chopped nuts
100g (3½oz) white chocolate, chopped

- Preheat the oven to 150°C/300°F/Gas 2. Grease a 25 x 15cm (10 x 6in) baking tin with butter.
- Cream the butter and sugar together, then beat in the eggs. Mix in the flour and cocoa. Stir in the chopped nuts and white chocolate pieces.
- Turn the mixture into the buttered tin. Bake for about 40 minutes for a sticky brownie or 50 minutes for a firmer result. Cut in the tin whilst still hot and remove when cool.

Summer

Summer Pudding with Real Vanilla Ice-cream

When I came to Britain in 1990, my first culinary shock was finding soggy bread with berries in it. What a horrible idea, I thought! But now this is my favourite way to finish a summer meal. When I was cooking at the Brasserie we used to make trays of summer pudding and serve it cut into squares. It was very popular. I prefer the traditional shape, in individual portions. If you don't have ramekins, use teacups. A spoonful of crème fraîche is all you need to complete this most English of desserts.

Serves 8
Preparation time: 40 minutes plus 4 hours cooling, churning and freezing

1.25kg (2¾lb) mixed summer berries (traditionally not including strawberries)
200g (7oz) caster sugar
16 thin slices white bread

For the ice-cream
500ml (17floz) double cream
500ml (17floz) whole milk
1 vanilla pod, split open
200g (7oz) caster sugar
10 egg yolks

- Mix the berries and sugar together in a saucepan and warm over a low heat until the berry juice starts to run. Turn the berry and sugar mixture into a sieve set over a bowl and allow the resulting dark red syrup to run into the bowl.
- Meanwhile, cut 16 circles of bread from the slices to fit the base of 8 ramekins or teacups, plus crustless strips to fit the sides.
- To assemble the puddings, dip half of the circles of bread in the released berry juice and place on the base of the ungreased ramekins or teacups. Line the sides with the strips, dipped into the juice. Spoon the berry mixture into the centre and then top with the remaining circles of bread, dipped in juice. Weight with a tray and refrigerate overnight or for at least 6 hours.
- To make the ice cream, put the cream, milk, vanilla pod and half the sugar in a heavy saucepan and bring almost to the boil. Meanwhile, beat the yolks with

the rest of the sugar in a bowl. Pour the hot cream mixture on to the egg yolks and stir to combine, then return to the pan. Cook over a low heat briefly, stirring, until thickened. Discard the vanilla pod. Allow to cool. When cold, churn in an electric ice-cream machine, following the manufacturer's instructions. Or, freeze in an ice tray, whisking the mixture every 20 minutes or so until it is set. Once set, leave the ice-cream in the freezer for about 4 hours.
- Unmould the puddings and serve with the vanilla ice-cream.

Wine note

The perfect match for summer pudding is a South African wine called Constantia, first made in the eighteenth century and recently revived. It is quite unlike any other sweet wine you'll ever try. Sadly, it is unavailable in the Europe at the moment due to excess potential alcohol, but if you know anyone going to South Africa, ingratiate yourself quickly!

Summer

Souffléed Crêpes with Apple Caramel Sauce

Say soufflé to anyone and they'll think of three-star restaurants and difficulty. In reality, soufflés aren't difficult – the version here is easy as anything, and the dish will impress your friends for very little risk. The crêpes can be made in the morning and stored in the fridge between layers of greaseproof paper.

Serves 4
Preparation time: 40 minutes
Cooking time: 7 minutes

For the crêpes
2 tablespoons caster sugar
1 egg
300ml (10floz) milk
115g (4oz) plain flour
butter for frying

For the filling
200g (7oz) cooking apples, peeled and cut into 1cm (½in) dice
200g (7oz) caster sugar
½ quantity pastry cream (see Deep Raspberry Tart, page 209)

For the sauce
1 litre (1¾ pints) clear apple juice

For the meringue
2 egg whites
2 tablespoons caster sugar
icing sugar to dust

- To make the crêpe batter, beat the sugar into the egg and add a little of the milk. Incorporate the flour, then thin with the rest of the milk. Allow to stand for 30 minutes.
- Using a 15cm (6in) crêpe pan, fry the crêpes in gently foaming butter. This quantity of batter will make about 8 crêpes. Choose the best 4 for this dessert.
- To make the filling, cook the apples with the sugar and 1 tablespoon water over a low heat until they start to soften. Set aside.
- To make the apple caramel sauce, boil the apple juice until reduced to about 100ml (3½floz). Set aside.

- Preheat the oven to 240°C/475°F/Gas 9 or its highest setting.
- For the meringue, beat the egg whites and sugar together to form stiff peaks.
- Place a tablespoon of the apple filling in the centre of each crêpe and add 2 tablespoons of pastry cream. Fold over in half and then fold again to make a triangle. Pipe the meringue into each of the folds and place on a greased baking tray. Bake for 7 minutes or until the meringue starts to brown.
- Flood 4 plates with the apple caramel sauce. Top each with a crêpe, dust with icing sugar and serve immediately.

Wine note

The sweet wines of the Loire, made from the Chenin Blanc grape, show the most appley of flavours. A sweet Vouvray of at least ten summers would be heaven.

Summer

Deep Raspberry Tart

Raspberries are my favourite fruit, and it is a great treat to have the first Scottish raspberries of the summer to make this dish. The tart is a real classic of French pâtisserie and is just as wonderful topped with any soft fruits that are in season. Alternatively, omit the fruit and sprinkle with flaked almonds before baking. This remains a firm favourite of my best friend, Peter, who has a world-class sweet tooth.

Serves 10
Preparation time: 30 minutes plus 3 hours chilling
Cooking time: 1 hour

a 21cm (8 ½ in) pastry case (see Rhubarb and Almond Cream Tart, page 200), baked blind
400g (14oz) raspberries
icing sugar to dust

For the pastry cream
500ml (17floz) whole milk
1 vanilla pod, split open
125g (4½oz) caster sugar
6 egg yolks
45g (1½oz) plain flour

- Preheat the oven to 180°C/350°F/Gas 4.
- To make the pastry cream, put the milk in a saucepan and scrape in the seeds from the vanilla pod. Add the pod itself and half of the sugar. Bring almost to the boil.
- Meanwhile, in a bowl, beat the egg yolks with the remaining sugar until light and fluffy. When the yolks lighten in colour you know they have been aerated and the sugar has dissolved. Beat in the flour.
- When the milk is hot, pour it over the eggs. (It is very important to add the milk to the yolks rather than the reverse. If you add the eggs to the hot milk the heat will scramble them instantly, whereas adding hot milk to eggs raises the temperature generally and the two mix easily.) Stir to combine, then return the mixture to the pan. Gently cook, stirring constantly, until the mixture is thick enough to hold a line dragged over the back of the stirring spoon. Discard the vanilla pod. (At this point, if more convenient, the pastry cream can be cooled and then kept in the fridge for a couple of days.)

- Pour the pastry cream into the pastry case. Bake for about 20 minutes or until when gently shaken the filling doesn't wobble. Remove to a wire rack and cool to room temperature. (Although both the pastry case and the filling can be made in advance, once cooked together the tart must never see the fridge or it will go soggy and stale very quickly.)
- Top the filling with raspberries and dust lightly with icing sugar.

Wine note

This is quite a robust dessert and, although not too sweet, the acidity of the raspberries demands a sturdy wine. An Australian botrytized Riesling or Semillon would be ideal.

Summer

Asian Pears with Chocolate Mousse and Pistachios

When I was at school, and then on summer break from varsity, I used to eat with a dear friend, Rhonda, in a restaurant called the Bayswater Café. Our culinary jaunts to 'the Bays' were formative in my appreciation of pure, simple food. Rhonda's mother, Yvonne, was a great cook and used to turn out the finest chocolate mousse. This recipe is hers.

Serves 8
Preparation time: 45 minutes plus cooling

For the pears
400ml (14floz) white wine
250g (9oz) caster sugar
1 vanilla pod, split open
8 Asian pears, peeled

For the chocolate mousse
250g (9oz) dark, bitter chocolate (at least 70% cocoa solids)
50g (scant 2oz) unsalted butter
3 eggs, separated
250ml (8½floz) double cream

To serve
100g (3½oz) flaked pistachios

- Combine the wine, sugar and vanilla pod in a saucepan with 1 litre (1¾ pints) water. Add the pears and poach for 12 minutes. (These pears are firm even when cooked and should retain a little bite so as not to cloy.) Allow to cool in the liquid.
- Drain the pears. Cut off the top third and scoop out the core. Set aside.
- Melt the chocolate in a bain-marie. Remove from the heat and stir in the butter and egg yolks (if the chocolate is too hot, the egg yolks will cook and go grainy).
- Whip the cream until it forms soft peaks, then fold through the chocolate mixture. Beat the egg whites until they too form soft peaks, and fold into the mixture. Pour into a bowl and put in the fridge to set.
- When ready to serve, pipe the chocolate mousse in a swirly pattern on to the pears and sprinkle with the flaked pistachios.

Summer

Pavlova with Passion fruit and Strawberries

Named for the ballerina Anna Pavlova, and just as light and dreamy, the 'pav' is an institution. The crunchy outside should give way to a gooey, hazelnutty interior with just enough cream for richness and tart fruits to give balance.

Serves 6
Preparation time: 20 minutes
Cooking time: 1 hour

400g (14oz) strawberries
250ml (8½floz) double cream
a few drops of pure vanilla essence
icing sugar to taste
6 passion fruits

pinch of salt
340g (12oz) caster sugar
1 teaspoon malt vinegar
1 teaspoon cornflour
1 teaspoon pure vanilla essence

For the meringue
6 egg whites

- Preheat the oven to 120°C/225°F/Gas ¼. Line an oven tray with baking parchment.
- Whisk the egg whites with the salt in a clean bowl until stiff. Slowly add the caster sugar, a tablespoon at a time, whisking constantly. Gently fold in the vinegar, cornflour and vanilla essence.
- Spoon the meringue on to the centre of the lined baking tray and form into a 25cm (10in) diameter round, using a rubber spatula to shape the sides and make a hollow in the centre. Bake for 1 hour. Set aside to cool on a wire rack.
- Purée half of the strawberries in a food processor; slice the remainder.
- Whip the cream with a few drops of vanilla essence and icing sugar to taste. Spread over the top of the cooled meringue. Pour over the strawberry purée, letting it trickle down the sides. Top with the strawberry slices and then the pulp from the passion fruits.

Autumn

'Punkin' Pie with Bourbon Cream and Candied Physalis

This is the best version of this American classic I've found, and is all the easier for not needing the pastry case to be baked blind. It may seem rather strange to make a pudding from a vegetable – although squashes are in fact botanically fruit – but the good quality squashes, such as kabocha and butternut, that we get now are really flavoursome and sweet. The bourbon cream re-emphasises the influence of the American South, and the physalis (also called cape gooseberry) brings the finished pudding up to date. If you would rather serve the pie whole at table with just the cream, that's fine.

Serves 8
Preparation time: 30 minutes plus 3 hours chilling
Cooking time: 1 hour

2 eggs
50g (scant 2oz) caster sugar
50g (scant 2oz) soft brown sugar
500g (1lb 2oz) cooked pumpkin or squash purée, fresh or canned
375ml (12½floz) evaporated milk or thick cream
pinch of salt
1 teaspoon ground cinnamon
½ teaspoon ground ginger
½ teaspoon freshly grated nutmeg
pinch of ground cloves

a 23cm (9in) pastry case (see Lime Tart with Passion Fruit Sauce, page 198)
icing sugar to dust

For the cream
450ml (15floz) double or whipping cream
100g (3½oz) caster sugar
100ml (3½floz) bourbon whisky

For the physalis garnish
200g (7oz) caster sugar
24 physalis

- Preheat the oven to 225°C/425°F/Gas 7.
- Beat the eggs with the caster sugar. Stir in the soft brown sugar, then add the pumpkin purée, evaporated milk, salt and spices.

- Fill the pastry case with the pumpkin mixture and bake for 15 minutes. Reduce the oven temperature to 190°C/375°F/Gas 5 and continue baking for 45 minutes. Allow to cool to room temperature.
- Meanwhile, make the bourbon cream. Whip the cream to a soft consistency, then gradually add the sugar as you continue to whip. Near the point that the cream starts to form firm peaks, add the bourbon in three or four amounts, whipping until amalgamated. The whisky will make the cream looser than ordinary whipped cream but all the more delicious!
- For the caramelized physalis, put the sugar in a saucepan with 150ml (5floz) water and slowly bring to the boil, without stirring. Once the water has evaporated, the sugar will start to cook and melt to become caramel. It is very important that there are no sugar crystals on the side of the pan or the caramel will crystallize. So to keep the caramel moving, to cook and colour it evenly, swirl it gently in the pan from time to time. When the caramel is uniform in colour (a light mahogany), remove from the heat.
- While the caramel cooks, fold the papery cases of the physalis back and twist into stems or handles. Grease a piece of foil with a little vegetable oil. Dip the fruits into the caramel, off the heat, and rest on the foil to set. The physalis will easily stand up and will harden in a matter of minutes. The caramel coating will stay firm and crunchy as long as the humidity around the physalis is not too high, so keep them away from the steam of the stove.
- To serve, dust the pie with icing sugar and accompany with the bourbon cream and physalis.

Wine note

The spicy denseness of the pumpkin pie suggests a sweet sherry like the excellent Matusalem from Gonzalez Byass, a sweet oloroso with amazing depth of flavour. It is now available in half bottles in supermarkets.

Autumn

Apple and Prune Cake with Lavender Ice-cream

The apple cake is a version of a recipe from those inestimable women, the two Fat Ladies, who made it for a village fête in their first TV series. Lavender ice-cream has been a favourite of mine for ages. I usually add juniper too, but have left out the gin scent in deference to Clarissa. Home-made cake and the smell of granny's hankies has more than a passing WI feel to it!

Serves 8
Preparation time: 20 minutes
Cooking time: 1 hour 5 minutes

For the cake
140g (5oz) butter
200g (7oz) plus 3 tablespoons caster sugar
2 eggs, well beaten
85g (3oz) self-raising flour
115g (4oz) ground almonds
120ml (4floz) milk
1 teaspoon pure vanilla essence
1 tablespoon boiling water
10 prunes, stoned and roughly chopped
2 green apples, skin on, cored and sliced
pinch of ground cinnamon

For the lavender ice-cream
500ml (17floz) double cream
500ml (17floz) whole milk
1 vanilla pod, split open
handful of dried or fresh lavender
200g (7oz) caster sugar
10 egg yolks

- First make the ice cream. Put the cream, milk, vanilla pod, lavender and half the sugar in a heavy saucepan and bring almost to the boil. Meanwhile, beat the yolks with the rest of the sugar in a bowl. Pour the hot cream mixture on to the egg yolks and stir to combine, then return to the pan. Cook over a low heat briefly, stirring, until thickened. Discard the vanilla pod. Allow to cool. When cold, churn in an electric ice-cream machine, following the manufacturer's

- instructions. Or, freeze in an ice tray, whisking the mixture every 20 minutes or so until it is set.
- Preheat the oven to 190°C/375°F/Gas 5. Grease and line a 25cm (10in) round cake tin.
- To make the cake, place the butter, 200g (7oz) sugar, eggs, flour, almonds, milk, vanilla essence and boiling water in a food processor and process until smooth and well mixed. Pour into the prepared tin. Scatter the prune pieces over the top, then arrange the apple slices on the prunes. Bake for 45 minutes.
- Sprinkle with the extra sugar and the cinnamon and bake for a further 20 minutes or until a skewer inserted into the centre of the cake comes out clean. Cool in the tin.
- Serve the cake while still warmish, with the ice-cream.

Autumn

Poached Pear with Lime Caramel Sauce

This is a dramatic dessert for special occasions, guaranteed to bring a 'wow!' from your guests. Making spun sugar is not as difficult as you might think, but if you are a bit worried about it, just leave it out. If you are going to make spun sugar, do it at the last moment because it will quickly soften in a hot, humid atmosphere – like that in a kitchen.

Serves 6
Preparation time: 30 minutes
Cooking time: 30 minutes

juice of 2 lemons
6 ripe, unblemished pears
500g (1lb 2oz) caster sugar
1 sheet ready-rolled puffed pastry, about 250g (9oz)
1 egg yolk, beaten
juice of 6 limes
250ml (8½floz) double cream

- Fill a bowl with water and add the lemon juice. Peel the pears, keeping them whole and with the stalks attached. As each pear is peeled, put it in the bowl of acidulated water.
- Put 250g (9oz) of the sugar in a saucepan large enough to hold all the pears and add 1 litre (1¾ pints) water. Bring to the boil, stirring to dissolve the sugar. Drain the pears and add to the pan of sugar syrup. Simmer gently until tender. This should take about 15 minutes, but depends enormously on the ripeness of the pears. Remove from the heat and leave the pears to cool in the syrup.
- Preheat the oven to 225°C/425°F/Gas 7.
- Lay the sheet of puff pastry on a lightly floured work surface and cut out 6 discs, each 8cm (3¼in) in diameter. With a 7cm (2¾in) round pastry cutter, mark a ring in the centre of each disc, 5mm (¼in) inside the edge all round. Glaze the surfaces of the discs with beaten egg yolk and transfer to a baking tray. Bake for

15 minutes or until golden brown. (A second glazing half-way through baking will ensure a deeper gloss.) Cool on a wire rack.
- Put 125g (4½oz) of the remaining sugar in a saucepan with a little water and slowly bring to the boil, without stirring. Once the water has evaporated, the sugar will start to cook and melt to become caramel. It is very important that there are no sugar crystals on the side of the pan or the caramel will crystallize. To keep the caramel moving, to cook and colour it evenly, swirl it gently in the pan from time to time. When the caramel is uniform in colour (a light mahogany), remove from the heat and add the lime juice – take care because the caramel will bubble and steam. Stir well. Stir in the cream and return to the heat to melt the caramel, if necessary. You should have a thick, glossy lime-scented sauce. Set aside.
- Put the remaining sugar in another saucepan with a little water and cook to a caramel as you did for the sauce. Cook the caramel until it is a uniform dark mahogany colour, then remove from the heat and allow to cool until a fork will pick up tiny strands. While waiting for the caramel to be cool enough to spin, set up an area with lots of kitchen paper on the floor and 2 wooden spoon handles (hold the bowls of the spoons under a board), 30cm (12in) apart, suspended over the paper.
- As soon as the caramel is ready to be spun, use 2 forks to flick the molten caramel over the 2 spoon handles to form thin strands that will solidify on contact with the cold air. Once a mass of strands has been thus thrown it can be gathered up and gently formed into a ball, then placed on a greased sheet of foil.
- To assemble the dessert, set a pastry case on each plate. Drain the pears and put one in each pastry case. Surround with the caramel cream sauce and top each pear with a small ball of spun sugar. Serve and wait for the compliments.

Wine note

A superb German sweet Riesling at beerenauslese or trockenbeerenauslese level would suit this perfectly.

Autumn

Rhubarb and Apple Charlotte

Charlottes are lovely puddings to make at the last minute, when unexpected visitors arrive, because they're so simple and yet so attractive. The rhubarb is gooey, but the apple gives it a better texture. I made a similar but fat-free version for a dinner given by The Sunday Times, *which tested fat-free dishes. It was so successful that thousands of people wrote in for recipe sheets.*

Serves 6
Preparation time: 30 minutes
Cooking time: 45 minutes

1 large stale white bread loaf
75g (2½oz) butter, softened
3 tablespoons icing sugar
450g (1lb) apples, cored and cubed
225g (8oz) rhubarb, cut into 2.5cm (1in) pieces
grated zest and juice of 1½ lemons
pinch of ground cinnamon
3 tablespoons caster sugar
50g (scant 2oz) breadcrumbs or cake crumbs
Crème Anglaise (see page 231) to serve

- Preheat the oven to 200°C/400°F/Gas 6.
- Slice the loaf of bread in half lengthways, then cut into thin slices. Remove all the crusts. Using about two-thirds of the butter, lightly butter the slices of bread on both sides. Coat one side of each slice with icing sugar. Toast all the bread under the grill on the sugared side until golden brown.
- Butter a 1.2 litre (2 pint) charlotte mould and line the bottom and the sides with the slices of toasted bread, toasted side out. Arrange them so that all the slices overlap slightly. Leave aside enough toasted bread for a lid for the charlotte.
- Put the rest of the butter in a saucepan with the apples, rhubarb and lemon zest and juice. Add the cinnamon and stir together over a low heat, cooking the apples and rhubarb very gently until they are soft. Make sure you cook them

uncovered so that they stay quite dry. When the apples and rhubarb are soft and fluffy, stir in the caster sugar and the breadcrumbs or cake crumbs.
- Spoon the fruit mixture into the bread-lined charlotte mould. Make a lid with the reserved toasted bread. Place the mould in a roasting tin two thirds filled with water. Bake in the centre of the oven for about 45 minutes.
- Loosen the edges with a knife and turn out the charlotte on to a dish. Serve hot with plenty of crème anglaise!

Wine note

The gentle flavours of this would be delicious with a sweet champagne such as Veuve Cliquot rich.

Winter

Apricot Strudel

Strudel is traditionally made with a special dough, stretched out thinly enough to read a newspaper through it, but I'd really rather be reading the paper than making the dough. This is an excellent use for bought filo pastry. The richness of dried apricots gives a wonderful intensity, and they can now be bought in a ready-to-use version that is too yummy for words.

Serves 4
Preparation time: 20 minutes
Cooking time: 10 minutes

170g (6oz) dried apricots
35g (generous 1oz) dried cranberries
1 tablespoon finely chopped stem ginger in syrup
2 tablespoons brandy or Calvados
2 sheets filo pastry
25g (scant 1oz) butter, melted
1 tablespoon icing sugar

- Gently simmer the apricots and cranberries with the ginger, brandy and 240ml (8floz) water for 5 minutes to plump up the fruit. Leave to cool, then gently press out any excess liquid from the fruit.
- Preheat the oven to 200°C/400°F/Gas 6.
- Brush one sheet of filo with a little of the melted butter and set the other sheet on top. Brush it with butter, then dredge with some of the icing sugar. Spoon the apricot filling down the length of the filo in a sausage shape, leaving a small border clear all round. Fold the short ends in, then fold in one long side. Brush with more butter and roll up. Brush the last edge with butter and seal. Carefully lift on to a buttered baking tray. Brush with the last of the butter and sprinkle with the remaining icing sugar.
- Bake for 10 minutes or until the pastry is golden brown and the wonderful smell starts to waft. Remove from the oven, slice at an angle and serve with Vanilla Ice-cream (see page 205).

Winter

Tiramisù with White Chocolate

The pudding of the late 1980s, tira mi sù, *or 'pick me up', is so ubiquitous that I half expect to see a 'just add water' version soon. In my recipe, layers of white chocolate give a luxurious crunch to the otherwise very soft traditional product. Mascarpone cheese is now available in supermarkets and, whilst it is a cream cheese, cream cheese itself is no substitue as it is too heavy. As this dish contains raw eggs, it is not suitable for the very old or very young or pregnant women. I don't know if it's the caffeine, sugar or alcohol that picks one up, but it does!*

Serves 4
Preparation time: 20 minutes plus 3 hours setting

2 eggs, separated
400g (14oz) mascarpone
60ml (2floz) brandy or Marsala
6 tablespoons icing sugar
120ml (4floz) very strong coffee

6 tablespoons dark rum
1 packet sponge finger biscuits
150g (5½oz) white chocolate, melted
cocoa powder to dust

- Beat the egg yolks into the mascarpone with the brandy or Marsala and icing sugar. Beat the egg whites until stiff and then fold in.
- Mix the coffee with the rum. Dip the biscuits into the mixture to moisten, then layer half of them, one deep, in a serving dish. Spread half of the mascarpone mixture over the biscuits and drizzle over half of the melted chocolate. Repeat the layers. Leave to cool and set.
- Dust with cocoa powder. Chill before serving.

Winter

Beetroot Chocolate Cake with Burnt Caramel Ice-cream

Although beetroot has a bad press in this country, I was brought up with it and this cake is a favourite of mine (obviously, don't use the pickled variety of beetroot). The way the beetroot works is to reinforce the very dark colour of the cake and provide the moisture of the mass, in the same way carrot works in a cake. When I was on the Big Breakfast, Vanessa Feltz and I had a running battle about beetroot. She hated it and I was forever trying to change her opinion. The only time I managed to get her to eat it was by combining it with her nemesis… chocolate, in this cake.

Serves 8
Preparation time: 30 minutes
Cooking time: 35 minutes

For the cake
85g (3oz) dark chocolate
3 eggs
300g (10½oz) sugar
240ml (8floz) sunflower oil
300g (10½oz) cooked beetroot, peeled and puréed
30g (1oz) cocoa powder
200g (7oz) plain flour
1½ teaspoons bicarbonate of soda

For the ganache
250g (9oz) dark chocolate
250ml (8½floz) double cream

For the ice-cream
125g (4½oz) caster sugar
5 egg yolks
250ml (8½floz) double cream
250ml (8½floz) milk

- Preheat the oven to 180°C/350°F/Gas 4. Grease and flour a 25cm (10in) springform cake tin.

- To make the cake, melt the chocolate in a bain-marie. Lightly beat the eggs with the sugar and oil, then gradually beat in the beetroot purée. Stir in the melted chocolate. Sift the cocoa, flour and bicarbonate of soda over the surface and mix in thoroughly.
- Spoon the cake mixture into the prepared tin and bake for 35 minutes or until the centre springs back when lightly pressed. Leave to cool on a wire rack.
- For the ganache, break up the chocolate into a heatproof bowl. Bring the cream almost to the boil, then pour over the chocolate. Beat together – the hot cream will melt the chocolate. Whilst the ganache is still hot, use it to ice the cake. Set aside to cool and harden.
- To make the ice-cream, put the sugar and a little water in a saucepan over a low heat and cook to a dark caramel sauce without stirring (this would crystallize the caramel). If darker spots appear, swirl the pan to mix them back in. Meanwhile, whisk the egg yolks in a bowl until fluffy.
- When the caramel has gone just past pleasant and is beginning to smell burnt, pour in the cream and then the milk. The caramel will harden. Lower the flame and continue to cook gently, stirring, until the caramel has dissolved into the cream and milk. Pour over the yolks, whisking well, then return to the pan. Gently cook, stirring constantly, until a line drawn on the back of the spoon holds. Immediately pour back into the egg yolk bowl to arrest the cooking. Leave to cool and then churn in an ice-cream machine, following manufacturer's instructions. Or pour into an ice tray and freeze, whisking every 20 minutes or so until set. Leave the ice-cream in the freezer for 4 hours before serving. Serve the ice-cream with the cake.

Wine note

Try a chilled 10- or 20-year-old tawny port.

Winter

Oatcakes and Chutney for Cheese

Home-made chutney and oatcakes lift cheese into a course fit for kings. There is nothing I enjoy more than serving members of other EC states British cheeses and leaving them to draw their own conclusions.

Makes 2 litres (3½ pints) chutney and about 20 oatcakes
Preparation time: 30 minutes
Cooking time: 2 hours

For the rhubarb and date chutney
1.8kg (4lb) rhubarb, chopped
450g (1lb) dates, stoned and finely chopped
450g (1lb) onions, finely chopped
1 tablespoon ground ginger
1 tablespoon mixed spice
1 teaspoon curry powder or 5-spice powder
1 teaspoon salt
450g (1lb) molasses
300ml (10floz) malt vinegar

For the oatcakes
340g (12oz) pinhead oatmeal
115g (4oz) butter
1 egg
pinch of salt

- Place all the ingredients for the chutney in a large non-reactive pan and gently simmer for 2 hours or until tender. Stir from time to time and add more vinegar if necessary. Remove from the heat and spoon into sterilized jars. Store in a dark cool cupboard. The chutney can be eaten immediately, but is much nicer if kept for 6 months.
- For the oatcakes, preheat the oven to 200°C/400°F/Gas 6.
- Mix all the ingredients together, adding enough water to form a softish dough. Roll out as thinly as possible and cut into 10cm (4in) rounds. Transfer to baking trays sprinkled with wholemeal flour. Bake for about 12 minutes or until dry to the touch but not coloured. Store in an airtight container.

Winter

Dark and White Chocolate Tart

This is really rich, yet it contains only a little sugar in the pastry. It was inspired by an excellent recipe published by the most feted chef in Britain, Marco-Pierre White. The tart will keep to the next day, but in its first day has a fantastic moussey nature that goes after a few hours. This is delicious with raspberries and crème fraîche. If you prefer, dust the tart with cocoa powder rather than drizzling with white chocolate.

Serves 10
Preparation time: 30 minutes plus 3 hours chilling
Cooking time: 50 minutes

500g (1lb 2oz) best-quality dark chocolate (at least 70% cocoa solids)
50g (scant 2oz) white chocolate
360ml (12floz) double cream
200ml (7floz) whole milk
thinly pared zest of 1 orange
3 eggs, lightly beaten
a 21cm (8½in) pastry case (see Rhubarb and Almond Cream Tart, page 200), baked blind

- Preheat the oven to 200°C/400°F/Gas 6.
- Melt the dark and white chocolates separately in bowls set over boiling water; watch the white chocolate closely as it scorches and then splits very quickly if overheated. Remove from the heat, but leave over the hot water.
- Bring the cream and milk almost to the boil with the orange zest, then strain over the eggs and stir to combine. Pour the melted dark chocolate slowly into the milk and egg mixture, stirring the whole time, and mix thoroughly into a homogeneous mass.
- Pour the dark chocolate mixture into the pastry case. Bake for about 30 minutes or until the centre of the filling only just wobbles. If the oven is too hot the filling will start to rise, like a soufflé, and will then have a cracked appearance on cooling.
- When cool, drizzle with the white chocolate.

BASIC
RECIPES

Béchamel Sauce

Makes 500ml (17floz)   Preparation time: 5 minutes   Cooking time: 7 minutes

50g (scant 2oz) butter
50g (scant 2oz) plain flour
500ml (17floz) whole milk

¼ teaspoon salt
freshly grated nutmeg

- Heat the butter in a heavy saucepan over a gentle heat until it liquifies. Mix in the flour. Cook the resulting paste (roux) for at least 4 minutes so there is no raw flour taste remaining, but do not colour the roux.
- In another saucepan, heat the milk to just under boiling point. Slowly add to the roux, keeping the mixture lump-free by beating after each addition. When all the milk has been added, and the sauce is thick and lump-free, season with the salt and nutmeg to taste.
- If not using immediately, place a buttered paper directly on the surface of the sauce to prevent a skin from forming.

Fresh Tomato Sauce

Makes 475ml (16floz)   Preparation time: 10 minutes   Cooking time: 40 minutes
1 large onion, finely chopped

4 garlic cloves, finely chopped
3 tablespoons olive oil
500g (1lb 2oz) fresh tomatoes, peeled and seeded, retaining the juices

15g (½oz) fresh oregano
salt and pepper

- Fry the onion and garlic in the oil until soft. Add the chopped tomatoes and cook over a low heat for 30 minutes, stirring occasionally.
- Season with salt and pepper and add the oregano leaves. Serve hot or allow to cool and store in the fridge or freezer.

Bread Sauce

This is more of a thin paste than a sauce and is delicious.

Serves 8   Preparation time: 5 minutes   Cooking time: 10 minutes

500ml (17floz) whole milk
1 onion, peeled and studded with 6 cloves
3 bay leaves

50g (scant 2oz) fresh white breadcrumbs (no crusts)
white pepper

- Put the milk in a saucepan with the onion and bay leaves. Simmer for 10 minutes to infuse the flavour into the milk. Remove the onion and bay leaves.
- Stir in the breadcrumbs and cook until a smooth and homogenous sauce is formed. Season with white pepper. Serve hot.

Basic Vinaigrette

For a lower-calorie version, add another tablespoon of Dijon mustard and gently beat in 100ml (3 1/2floz) water. This has none of the artificial flavours of bought lo-cal vinaigrettes, and the mustard helps it emulsify.

Makes 300ml (10floz)   Preparation time: 5 minutes

0ml (2floz) white wine vinegar
1 tablespoon Dijon mustard
1 tablespoon caster sugar

pinch of salt
pinch of freshly ground pepper
250ml (8 1/2floz) olive oil

- Mix together the vinegar, mustard, sugar, salt and pepper in a bowl or jug. Whisk in the oil until emulsified.
- If not using immediately, pour into a screw-topped jar and store in the fridge, shaking the dressing well before use.

Basic Mayonnaise

Olive oil alone is too strong for mayonnaise, but 60ml (2floz) of the sunflower oil can be replaced by olive oil or by walnut or any other flavoured oil. This is unsuitable for the very old, very young or pregnant women as it contains raw eggs.

Makes scant 300ml (10floz)   Preparation time: 5 minutes

2 egg yolks
2 teaspoons white wine vinegar
2 teaspoons Dijon mustard
2 teaspoons caster sugar
250ml (8½floz) sunflower oil
salt and black pepper

- Whisk the egg yolks, vinegar, mustard and sugar with a good pinch each of salt and black pepper. Slowly whisk in the oil until you have a stiff and glossy mass.
- If not using immediately, press cling film directly on to the surface of the mayonnaise, into the mixture (to stop oxidization), and then cover again with more cling film. Keep in the fridge.

Sauce Vierge

The 'vierge' refers to the raw tomatoes, rather than the olive oil.

Makes about 240ml (8floz)   Preparation time: 10 minutes plus 20 minutes infusing

100ml (3½floz) extra virgin olive oil
15g (½oz) fresh basil leaves, finely shredded
15g (½oz) fresh tarragon leaves
½ teaspoon coriander seeds
1 teaspoon balsamic vinegar
2 beef tomatoes, peeled, seeded and cut into 1cm (½in) dice
salt and pepper

- Warm the oil and stir in the herbs, seeds and vinegar. Season with salt and vinegar. Stir in the tomatoes.
- Leave to infuse for 20 minutes before serving.

Crème Anglaise

This runny custard was taught to the French by the English in the eighteenth century.

Makes 600ml (1 pint)   Preparation time: 5 minutes   Cooking time: 10 minutes

600ml (1 pint) whole milk
1 vanilla pod, split open

125g (4½oz) caster sugar
6 egg yolks

- Combine the milk, vanilla pod and half the sugar in a heavy saucepan and bring almost to the boil.
- Meanwhile, in a bowl, beat the egg yolks with the remaining sugar until light and fluffy.
- Pour the hot milk on to the yolks and, when well amalgamated, return to the pan and set over a gentle heat. Cook, stirring constantly and well, especially the sides of the pan, until the consistency of the custard is like double cream. Do not overheat or the egg yolks will scramble.
- Pour into a clean bowl, stir well and allow to cool. Keep, covered, in the fridge.

Tamarind Water

Tamarind water can be frozen, and used in many delicious dishes such as Chicken and Tamarind Salad (see page 98).

Makes 1 litre (1¾ pints)   Preparation time: 2 minutes

500g (1lb 2oz) tamarind pulp (with seeds)

- Cover the tamarind pulp with 1 litre (1¾ pints) of boiling water and leave to cool.
- Strain the tamarind water from the thickish paste. Keep in the refrigerator.

Basic Pasta Dough

Makes 500g (1lb 2oz)   Preparation time: 5 minutes

500g (1lb 2oz) strong white flour
pinch of salt
3 eggs
1 tablespoon olive oil

- Blend the flour with the salt, eggs and oil to make a mixture like sticky breadcrumbs. Add about 1 tablespoon water slowly to bind to a soft dough that can be formed into a ball. Leave to rest for 1 hour.
- Dust the pasta dough with flour, then knead and roll through a pasta machine, following the manufacturer's instructions.

Red Wine Jus

Makes 400ml (14floz)   Preparation time: 15 minutes   Cooking time: 3½ hours

2kg (4½lb) veal and/or chicken bones
3 large onions, unpeeled, roughly chopped
6 carrots, roughly chopped
1 bunch celery, roughly chopped
200ml (7floz) port
1 bottle red wine
1 bulb garlic, sliced horizontally in half
bunch of fresh thyme
bunch of parsley stalks
4 tomatoes
a few black peppercorns
salt and pepper

- Preheat the oven to 230°C/450°F/Gas 8. Put the bones in a roasting tin, roast for 30 minutes. Discard the fat. Transfer the bones to a large pot.
- Set the roasting tin over a moderate heat. Add the vegetables to the tin and cook briskly, stirring, to colour. Add the vegetables to the pot containing the bones and cover with water. Bring to the boil.
- Deglaze the tin with the port. Reduce by half, then add the red wine. Scrape up the residues and add to the pot with the garlic, herbs, tomatoes, peppercorns and seasoning. Bring to the boil and skim. Simmer for 3 hours, skimming often. Strain into a small pan, discard the solids. Reduce to 400ml (14floz).
- Keep in the fridge for 3 days.

Focaccia

This can be topped with herbs, artichokes or courgette slices, or baked plain, with salt, as here. It goes stale quickly, so is best served fresh and warm.

Makes 1   Preparation time: 5 minutes plus 1 hour rising   Cooking time: 25 minutes

25g (scant 1oz) dried yeast
15g (½oz) caster sugar
500g (1lb 2oz) strong plain flour
pinch of salt

4 teaspoons olive oil, plus more for sprinkling
flaked Maldon sea salt

- Mix the yeast and sugar into 240ml (8floz) of lukewarm water and allow to bubble for 15 minutes.
- Sift the flour into a large bowl and add the salt. Work the yeast mixture into the flour, adding the oil and any additional water that might be needed to produce a smooth and soft dough. Knead well for 10 minutes using a dough hook or by hand. Cover and leave to rise in a warm place for 1 hour.
- Preheat the oven to 240°C/475°F/Gas 9 or its highest setting.
- Knock back the dough. Turn it on to an oiled baking tray and press out into a rectangle about 20 x 28cm (8 x 11in). Make holes all over the surface with a finger, then sprinkle with olive oil and flaked salt. Bake for 25 minutes.

Sloe Gin

When the sloe gin is ready to drink use the drained-off sloes to make a venison daube (see page 165).

Makes 1 litre (1¾ pints)   Preparation time: 5 minutes plus 9–12 months maturing

1kg (2¼lb) sloes
1kg (2¼lb) caster sugar

1 litre gin (1¾ pints) (any brand)

- Either freeze the sloes so they pop, or prick each one with a pin. Mix the sloes with the sugar and gin in a large jar or bottle. Cover to make airtight, then store in a dark, cool place for at least 9 months, preferably a year.
- Every time you go past, give the jar/bottle a shake. Strain before use.

MENUS

There are obviously many considerations for mapping out a menu when planning to entertain your friends – the budget, the time of year and the weather. How many are you expecting and how much help will you get? Will it be possible to make much in advance?

With each of the following menus I've tried to give an idea of balance to the dishes chosen, so that the first and main courses aren't both made of chicken or both highly spiced, for example. It's important to introduce a little light and shade by having cold and hot, sharp and sweet, and soft and crunchy. A typical Thai meal shows how this can be done very effectively. It usually consists of one course, where each dish is structured to complement the next one presented. Typically there is plain rice with salad, a curry, a soup, a deep-fried dish and pickles. Fruit finishes the meal.

As a guide, it is always better to prepare an easy or less expensive dish than to try to be overly elaborate. It wouldn't do to run out, or to bankrupt yourself, nor do you want to be so exhausted that you never try to cook for friends again. Just remember that it is your guests who are important, and that if you make a simple meal you'll have more time with them.

Wine Buffs' Menu

This is for serious wine buffs, with very traditional dishes that are chosen to support the wines and not overwhelm them. If drinking the best from your cellar, aim for plainer food and let the vinous pleasures reveal themselves.

Smoked salmon blinis

•

Potted shrimps

•

Beef fillet with red wine jus and wild mushrooms

•

24 carat brûlée

Mediterranean Menu

This Mediterranean menu is for a less formal occasion, where the emphasis is on strong flavours to evoke the heat of the sun. Most of the preparation for this could be done in advance, so it is ideal for busy foodies.

Pitta crisps with houmous and tahini yogurt

•

Sauté of chorizo, prawns and beans

•

Wild boar sauce for noodles

•

Deep Raspberry Tart

Vegetarian Menu

Vegetarian menus suit many people, but many products, such as bought pastry and curry pastes, many wines and cheeses, and Worcestershire sauce and fish sauce, are not vegetarian. Do also check if your guests eat eggs.

Chick pea fritters with carrot shreds

●

Chicory, aubergine and goat's cheese gratin
Plantain and spinach curry
Onion bhajias with coriander chutney
Vegetable couscous

●

Lime tart with passion fruit sauce

Kosher Menu

The food laws concerning kosher meals are very complex. There should be no mixing of meat and dairy products, no fish without fins and scales, and no blood. This is a meat-based meal. None of the canapés in this book conform, but crisps and salsa would be good instead.

White radish cake with bean sprouts and spring onions

●

Loin of lamb with artichokes
Latkes
Pattypan squash braised with rosemary and white wine

●

Fresh fruit

Middle Eastern Menu

The Middle Eastern meal is becoming very fashionable and the ingredients are readily available. Authenticity in this case would possibly be less desirable, but by matching the flavours carefully the right effect can be achieved. The watermelon salad is a very refreshing course between the two other highly spiced dishes.

Moroccan fishcakes and harissa

•

Watermelon, chicory and feta salad

•

Long-cooked leg of lamb in red wine

•

Dark and white chocolate tart

Fusion Menu

The new fusion cuisine presents many possibilities. As long as a balance is maintained and there are no jarring combinations, it is possible to go wild! The diverse combinations do work.

Moroccan bread pinwheels

•

Warm salad of black pudding and apples

•

Chargrilled tuna loin with salsa verde and tapenade

•

Beetroot chocolate cake with burnt caramel ice-cream

Thai Menu

For larger numbers in the summer, a Thai banquet is often a great idea, as the balance of dishes is often too much food for 6 or so. It is also ideal outdoor food with a few cold beers.

Thai roast duck curry
Chicken and tamarind salad
Pad Thai
Plain rice
Beancurd crab rolls with sweet chilli dip
White radish cake with bean sprouts and spring onions

•

Steamed squash with coconut and ginger custard
Asian peas with chocolate mousse and pistachios

Italian Buffet Menu

Even in winter, an indoor Italian buffet for a large number is a good idea!

Chicken fricassee with lemons and rosemary
Squid stuffed with its tentacles and prawns, red wine sauce
Root vegetable gratin
Spinach and ricotta malfatti
Stuffed vegetables
Salad of artichokes, quail's eggs and pecorino

•

Tiramisù with white chocolate

INDEX

A
almonds:
    Moroccan fishcakes and harissa, 17
    rhubarb and almond cream tart, 200-1
anchovies, 71-2
antipasto with pickled aubergines and Stromboli, 44-5
apples:
    apple and prune cake with lavender ice-cream, 215-16
    pheasant with Calvados and, 127
    rhubarb and apple charlotte, 219-20
    roast duck with prune and apple stuffing, 110-11
    souffléed crêpes with apple caramel sauce, 207-8
    warm salad of black pudding and, 54
apricots:
    apricot strudel, 221
    boned chicken with pecans and, 101-2
artichokes:
    fillet of beef with summer salad, 149-50
    guinea fowl supreme on an artichoke cake, 105-6
    loin of lamb with, 142-3
    Roman fried artichokes, 177
    salad of artichokes, quail's eggs and pecorino, 40
    tarte Tatin niçoise, 26-7
Asian pears with chocolate mousse and pistachios, 211
asparagus:
    chicken and mozzarella rolls with saffron mayo, 107-8
    fillet of beef with summer salad, 149-50
    smoked quail and asparagus salad with polenta chips, 99-100
    turbot with peas, broad beans and, 64
aubergines:
    antipasto with pickled aubergines and Stromboli, 44-5
    baba ganouj, 9-10
    chicory, aubergine and goat's cheese gratin, 55-6
    lentil moussaka, 189-90
    roasted pepper and aubergine terrine, 36-7
    supreme of chicken with aubergine fritters and bean salad, 103-4
    Thai roast duck curry, 124
    yellow curry of aubergines, 195
authentic pork vindaloo, 146-7
avocados:
    spice-crusted pork fillet, lentil salad and, 144-5
    tartlets of avocado mousse and quail's eggs, 15

B
baba ganouj, 9-10
baby potatoes and caviar, 12
bacon:
    cassoulet, 117-19
    venison daube with sloes, 165
    see also pancetta
basil:
    sauce vierge, 230
    tomato and basil tart, 185
beancurd crab rolls with sweet chilli dip, 7-8
beans:
    cassoulet, 117-19
    supreme of chicken with aubergine fritters and bean salad, 103-4
bean sprouts:
    stir-fry of duck and scallops, 134
    white radish cake with spring onions and, 179-80
béchamel sauce, 228
beef:
    beef fillet with red wine jus and wild mushrooms, 163-4
    fillet of beef with summer salad, 149-50
beetroot:
    beetroot chocolate cake with burnt caramel ice-cream, 223-4
    sea bass roll with beetroot gnocchi, 93-4
    smoked eel on latkes with rocket and beetroot relish, 84-5
bhajias, onion, 192
biscuits:
    oatcakes, 225
bisque, lobster, 58
black beans, smoked cod's roe with pak choi and, 95
black pudding:
    chicken legs stuffed with chestnuts and, 121-2
    warm salad of apples and, 54
blinis:
    potato, 91-2
    smoked salmon, 20-1
bouillabaise with rouille, 73-4
Bourbon cream, 213-14
bread:
    antipasto with pickled aubergines and Stromboli, 44-5
    bread sauce, 229
    focaccia, 233
    Moroccan bread pinwheels, 11
    panzanella, 33

poori, 9-10
rhubarb and apple charlottes, 219-20
summer pudding with real vanilla ice-cream, 205-6
tarragon chicken with mushroom 'boxes', 132-3
broad beans:
   fillet of beef with summer salad, 149-50
   hake in Serrano ham with capers and saffron pasta, 89-90
   sauté of chorizo, prawns and beans, 31-2
   turbot with peas, asparagus and, 64
brownies, wicked chocolate, 204
Brussels sprouts:
   sprout and chestnut soup with truffle oil, 57
buffet menu, 240
butter beans:
   supreme of chicken with aubergine fritters and bean salad, 103-4
butterflied leg of lamb with juniper, walnut oil and oregano, 148

C

cabbage *see* red cabbage
cakes:
   apple and prune cake with lavender ice-cream, 215-16
   beetroot chocolate cake with burnt caramel ice-cream, 223-4
   wicked chocolate brownies, 204
Calvados, pheasant with apples and, 127
canapés, 5-22
candied physalis, 213-14
cannelloni of hare and thyme, 166-7
capers, hake in Serrano ham with saffron pasta and, 89-90
caramel:
   burnt caramel ice-cream, 223-4
   poached pear with lime caramel sauce, 217-18
   souffléed crêpes with apple caramel sauce, 207-8
   24 carat brûlée, 202
carrot shreds, chick pea fritters with, 22
cassoulet, 117-19
caviar:
   baby potatoes and, 12
   vichyssoise with oyster and, 24
celeriac crisps with finnan sashimi, 16
champ, lamb shanks in red wine with, 155-6
chanterelles:
   beef fillet with red wine jus and wild mushrooms, 163-4
chargrilled tuna loin with salsa verde and tapenade, 71-2
charlotte, rhubarb and apple, 219-20
cheese:
   antipasto with pickled aubergines and Stromboli, 44-5
   chicken and mozzarella rolls with saffron mayo, 107-8
   chicory, aubergine and goat's cheese gratin, 55-6
   courgette, pea and mint pie, 176
   grandmother's handkerchiefs, 172-3
   Moroccan bread pinwheels, 11
   oatcakes and chutney for cheese, 225
   Parmesan wafers, 46-7
   red onion, feta and pine nut pizza, 181
   roasted pepper and aubergine terrine, 36-7
   Roquefort parfait with chestnut honey, 25
   salad of artichokes, quail's eggs and pecorino, 40
   spinach and ricotta malfatti, 34-5
   stuffed courgette flowers, 178
   Swiss chard fritters, 188
   watermelon, chicory and feta salad, 41
chervil butter sauce, tortellini of crab with, 65-6
chestnuts:
   chicken legs stuffed with black pudding and, 121-2
   pork chops with sherry and, 162
   sprout and chestnut soup with truffle oil, 57
   stress-free Christmas turkey, 135-6
chicken:
   boned chicken with apricots and pecans, 101-2
   chicken and mozzarella rolls with saffron mayo, 107-8
   chicken and tamarind salad, 98
   chicken fricassee with lemons and rosemary, 130-1
   chicken legs stuffed with chestnuts and black pudding, 121-2
   coronation chicken with shredded chicory, 112
   jambalaya, 109
   supreme of chicken with aubergine fritters and bean salad, 103-4
   tarragon chicken with mushroom 'boxes', 132-3
   velvet chicken with pineapple rice, 128-9
chicken liver parfait with caramelized orange, 38-9
chick peas:
   chick pea fritters with carrot shreds, 22
   mackerel and chick pea stew, 96
   mushroom filo pie, 184
   pitta crisps with houmous and tahini yogurt, 19
   tartlets of avocado mousse and quail's eggs, 15
chicory:
   chicory, aubergine and goat's cheese gratin, 55-6
   coronation chicken with shredded chicory, 112
   John Dory with chicory and tarragon sabayon, 80
   Thai seafood salad in chicory, 6
   watermelon, chicory and feta salad, 41
chillies:
   authentic pork vindaloo, 146-7
   Mexican-style loin of pork, 151-2
   pork-stuffed mild chillies, 18
   rouille, 73-4
   sweet chilli dipping sauce, 14
   Thai yellow bean cakes with tamarind dip, 175

trout fillet with oregano crust and smoked chilli sauce, 75-6
chives:
    mustard and chive sabayon, 52-3
chocolate:
    Asian pears with chocolate mousse and pistachios, 211
    beetroot chocolate cake with burnt caramel ice-cream, 223-4
    dark and white chocolate tart, 226
    Sicilian hare with chocolate, 168
    tiramisù with white chocolate, 222
    wicked chocolate brownies, 204
chorizo:
    jambalaya, 109
    sauté of prawns, beans and, 31-2
chutney:
    coriander chutney, 192
    rhubarb and date chutney, 225
cider:
    pheasant braised in cider, 120
    pheasant with Calvados and apples, 127
citrus basil dressing, 91-2
coconut milk:
    crab risotto with coriander and, 67
    plantain and spinach curry, 191
    Singaporean lakhsa, 83
    steamed squash with coconut and ginger custard, 203
    Thai roast duck curry, 124
    yellow curry of aubergines, 195
cod:
    steamed cod with ginger and rice wine, 88
cod's roe:
    smoked cod's roe with pak choi and black beans, 95
coffee:
    tiramisù with white chocolate, 222
confit of duck, 115-16
coriander:
    coriander chutney, 192
    crab risotto with coconut milk and, 67
    salsa verde, 71-2
coronation chicken with shredded chicory, 112
courgette flowers, stuffed, 178
courgettes:
    courgette, pea and mint pie, 176
    loin of lamb with artichokes, 142-3
couscous, vegetable, 186-7
crab:
    beancurd crab rolls with sweet chilli dip, 7-8
    crab risotto with coconut milk and coriander, 67
    tortellini of crab with chervil butter sauce, 65-6
cream, Bourbon, 213-14
crème anglaise, 231
crème brûlée, 24 carat, 202
crêpes:
    souffléed crêpes with apple caramel sauce, 207-8

cucumber:
    salmon steak with sautéed cucumbers and mint, 79
curries:
    authentic pork vindaloo, 146-7
    plantain and spinach curry, 191
    Thai roast duck curry, 124
    yellow curry of aubergines, 195
custard:
    coconut and ginger, 203
    crème anglaise, 231

D
dark and white chocolate tart, 226
dates:
    rhubarb and date chutney, 225
daube, venison with sloes, 165
dill blinis, 19
dressings:
    basic vinaigrette, 229
    citrus basil, 91-2
duck:
    cassoulet, 117-19
    duck and ginger wontons, 14
    roast duck with prune and apple stuffing, 110-11
    roast mallard, cooked two ways, 115-16
    stir-fry of duck and scallops, 134
    Thai roast duck curry, 124

E
eel *see* smoked eel
eggs:
    salad of artichokes, quail's eggs and pecorino, 40
    tartlets of avocado mousse and quail's eggs, 15

F
finnan haddock *see* smoked haddock
fish, 61-96
    bouillabaise with rouille, 73-4
    fish sausages with sauce vierge, 86-7
    Moroccan fishcakes and harissa, 17
    see also cod, salmon *etc*
focaccia, 233
French beans:
    French bean salad with tarator sauce, 183
    supreme of chicken with aubergine fritters and bean salad, 103-4
fritters:
    aubergine, 103-4
    chick pea, 22
    sweetcorn, 193-4
    Swiss chard, 188
fruit:
    summer pudding with real vanilla ice-cream, 205-6
    see also apples, strawberries *etc*
fusion menu, 239

G

game and poultry, 97-136
gin, sloe, 233
ginger:
    duck and ginger wontons, 14
    steamed cod with rice wine and, 88
    steamed squash with coconut and ginger custard, 203
gnocchi:
    sea bass roll with beetroot gnocchi, 93-4
    spinach and ricotta malfatti, 34-5
goat's cheese:
    chicory, aubergine and goat's cheese gratin, 55-6
    Moroccan bread pinwheels, 11
grandmother's handkerchiefs, 172-3
gratins:
    chicory, aubergine and goat's cheese, 55-6
    root vegetable, 196
gravadlax, 91-2
guinea fowl:
    guinea fowl, leek and potato terrine, 29-30
    guinea fowl supreme on an artichoke cake, 105-6
    guinea fowl with lime and moneybags, 113-14

H

haddock *see* smoked haddock
hake in Serrano ham with capers and saffron pasta, 89-90
ham:
    grandmother's handkerchiefs, 172-3
    hake in Serrano ham with capers and saffron pasta, 89-90
hare:
    cannelloni of thyme and, 166-7
    Sicilian hare with chocolate, 168
haricot beans:
    cassoulet, 117-19
harissa, Moroccan fishcakes and, 17
honey:
    Roquefort parfait with chestnut honey, 25
houmous, pitta crisps with tahini yogurt and, 19

I

ice-cream:
    burnt caramel, 223-4
    lavender, 215-16
    real vanilla, 205-6
Italian buffet menu, 240

J

jambalaya, 109
John Dory with chicory and tarragon sabayon, 80
juniper berries:
    butterflied leg of lamb with walnut oil, oregano and, 148
    pork with porcini and, 157

K

kidneys:
    kidneys with green peppercorns and fresh noodles, 169-70
    saddle of lamb stuffed with spinach and shiitakes, 138-9
kosher menu, 238

L

lakhsa, Singaporean, 83
lamb:
    butterflied leg of lamb with juniper, walnut oil and oregano, 148
    cassoulet, 117-19
    lamb shanks in red wine with champ, 155-6
    loin of lamb with artichokes, 142-3
    long-cooked leg of lamb in red wine, 158-9
    saddle of lamb stuffed with spinach and shiitakes, 138-9
latkes, smoked eel on, 84-5
lavender ice-cream, 215-16
leeks:
    guinea fowl, leek and potato terrine, 29-30
    vichyssoise with oyster and caviar, 24
lemons, chicken fricassee with rosemary and, 130-1
lentils:
    lentil moussaka, 189-90
    spice-crusted pork fillet, lentil salad and avocado, 144-5
lime:
    guinea fowl with moneybags and, 113-14
    lime tart with passion fruit sauce, 198-9
    poached pear with lime caramel sauce, 217-18
liver:
    chicken liver parfait with caramelized orange, 38-9
lobster bisque, 58
long-cooked leg of lamb in red wine, 158-9

M

mackerel and chick pea stew, 96
malfatti, spinach and ricotta, 34-5
mallard:
    roast mallard, cooked two ways, 115-16
mangoes:
    coronation chicken with shredded chicory, 112
mascarpone:
    smoked fish terrine and samphire salad, 69-70
    tiramisù with white chocolate, 222
mayonnaise:
    basic mayonnaise, 230
    saffron mayonnaise, 107-8
meat, 137-70
Mediterranean menu, 237
menus, 235-40
meringues:

pavlova with passion fruit and strawberries, 212
soufflèd crêpes with apple caramel sauce, 207-8
Mexican-style loin of pork, 151-2
Middle Eastern menu, 239
mint, salmon steak with sautéed cucumbers and, 79
moneybags, 113-14
mooli *see* white radishes
Moroccan bread pinwheels, 11
Moroccan fishcakes and harissa, 17
moussaka, lentil, 189-90
mousses:
    avocado, 15
    chocolate, 211
mung beans:
    Thai yellow bean cakes with tamarind dip, 175
mushrooms:
    beef fillet with red wine jus and wild mushrooms, 163-4
    mushroom filo pie, 184
    parsnip and porcini soup with mustard and chive sabayon, 52-3
    pork with juniper and porcini, 157
    rabbit and shiitake terrine, 50-1
    saddle of lamb stuffed with spinach and shiitakes, 138-9
    tarragon chicken with mushroom `boxes', 132-3
mussels, saffron broth of spring herbs and, 62-3
mustard:
    glazed smoked haddock with mustard cream, 68
    mustard and chive sabayon, 52-3

N

noodles:
    hake in Serrano ham with capers and saffron pasta, 89-90
    kidneys with green peppercorns and fresh noodles, 169-70
    pad thai, 42-3
    Singaporean lakhsa, 83
    wild boar sauce for noodles, 160-1

O

oatcakes, 225
olives:
    tapenade, 71-2
    tarte Tatin niçoise, 26-7
onions:
    mushroom filo pie, 184
    onion bhajias with coriander chutney, 192
    red onion, feta and pine nut pizza, 181
oranges:
    chicken liver parfait with caramelized orange, 38-9
    Mexican-style loin of pork, 151-2
    smoked quail and asparagus salad with polenta chips, 99-100
oregano:
    trout fillet with oregano crust and smoked chilli sauce, 75-6
oysters, vichyssoise with caviar and, 24

P

pad thai, 42-3
pak choi, smoked cod's roe with black beans and, 95
pancakes:
    grandmother's handkerchiefs, 172-3
pancetta:
    porcini risotto, 48-9
panzanella, 33
parfaits *see* pâtés
Parma ham:
    grandmother's handkerchiefs, 172-3
Parmesan wafers, 46-7
parsley pesto, 101-2
parsnip and porcini soup with mustard and chive sabayon, 52-3
partridges in red cabbage, 123
passion fruit:
    lime tart with passion fruit sauce, 198-9
    pavlova with strawberries and, 212
pasta:
    basic pasta dough, 232
    cannelloni of hare and thyme, 166-7
    hake in Serrano ham with capers and saffron pasta, 89-90
    kidneys with green peppercorns and fresh noodles, 169-70
    tortellini of crab with chervil butter sauce, 65-6
pâtés:
    chicken liver parfait with caramelized orange, 38-9
    Roquefort parfait with chestnut honey, 25
pattypan squash braised with rosemary and white wine, 182
pavlova with passion fruit and strawberries, 212
pears:
    Asian pears with chocolate mousse and pistachios, 211
    poached pear with lime caramel sauce, 217-18
peas:
    courgette, pea and mint pie, 176
    hake in Serrano ham with capers and saffron pasta, 89-90
    turbot with broad beans, asparagus and, 64
pecan nuts:
    boned chicken with apricots and, 101-2
    pheasant breast with sausage and pecan stuffing, thyme jus, 125-6
peppercorns:
    kidneys with green peppercorns and fresh noodles, 169-70
peppers:
    panzanella, 33

pepper-lined timbales, 86-7
roasted pepper and aubergine terrine, 36-7
salsa, 193-4
squid stuffed with its tentacles and prawns, red wine sauce, 81-2
tarte Tatin niçoise, 26-7
pesto, parsley, 101-2
pheasant:
  pheasant braised in cider, 120
  pheasant breast with sausage and pecan stuffing, thyme jus, 125-6
  pheasant with Calvados and apples, 127
physalis, candied, 213-14
pies:
  courgette, pea and mint pie, 176
  mushroom filo pie, 184
pine nuts:
  red onion, feta and pine nut pizza, 181
pineapple rice, velvet chicken with, 128-9
pistachios, Asian pears with chocolate mousse and, 211
pitta crisps with houmous and tahini yogurt, 19
pizza, red onion, feta and pine nut, 181
plantain and spinach curry, 191
polenta chips, smoked quail and asparagus salad with, 99-100
pommes Anna, 71-2
pommes fondants, 163-4
poori, 9-10
porcini:
  parsnip and porcini soup with mustard and chive sabayon, 52-3
  porcini risotto, 48-9
  pork with juniper and porcini, 157
pork:
  authentic pork vindaloo, 146-7
  Mexican-style loin of pork, 151-2
  pork chops with chestnuts and sherry, 162
  pork-stuffed mild chillies, 18
  pork with juniper and porcini, 157
  spice-crusted pork fillet, lentil salad and avocado, 144-5
port sauce, rabbit on watercress with, 140-1
potatoes:
  baby potatoes and caviar, 12
  guinea fowl, leek and potato terrine, 29-30
  lamb shanks in red wine with champ, 155-6
  pommes Anna, 71-2
  pommes fondants, 163-4
  potato blinis, gravadlax and citrus basil dressing, 91-2
  sea bass roll with beetroot gnocchi, 93-4
  smoked eel on latkes with rocket and beetroot relish, 84-5
  vichyssoise with oyster and caviar, 24
potted shrimps, 28
poultry and game, 97-136

prawns:
  prawn tempura with wasabi, 13
  sauté of chorizo, prawns and beans, 31-2
  Singaporean lakhsa, 83
  squid stuffed with its tentacles and prawns, red wine sauce, 81-2
pressed ox tongue, my grandmother's way, 153-4
prunes:
  apple and prune cake with lavender ice-cream, 215-16
  roast duck with prune and apple stuffing, 110-11
puddings, 197-226
pumpkin:
  `punkin' pie with Bourbon cream and candied physalis, 213-14

Q
quail *see* smoked quail
quail's eggs:
  salad of artichokes, pecorino and, 40
  tartlets of avocado mousse and, 15

R
rabbit:
  rabbit and shiitake terrine, 50-1
  rabbit on watercress with a port sauce, 140-1
raspberry tart, 209-10
red cabbage, partridges in, 123
red wine jus, 232
relish, beetroot, 84-5
rhubarb:
  rhubarb and almond cream tart, 200-1
  rhubarb and apple charlotte, 219-20
  rhubarb and date chutney, 225
rice:
  crab risotto with coconut milk and coriander, 67
  guinea fowl supreme on an artichoke cake, 105-6
  jambalaya, 109
  porcini risotto, 48-9
  velvet chicken with pineapple rice, 128-9
rice wine, steamed cod with ginger and, 88
risotto:
  crab risotto with coconut milk and coriander, 67
  porcini risotto, 48-9
rocket, smoked eel on latkes with, 84-5
roes:
  smoked cod's roe with pak choi and black beans, 95
Roman fried artichokes, 177
root vegetable gratin, 196
Roquefort parfait with chestnut honey, 25
rosemary:
  chicken fricassee with lemons and, 130-1
  pattypan squash braised with white wine and, 182
rouille, bouillabaise with, 73-4

S

sabayon:
   mustard and chive, 52-3
   tarragon, 80
saffron:
   chicken and mozzarella rolls with saffron mayo, 107-8
   hake in Serrano ham with capers and saffron pasta, 89-90
   saffron broth of mussels and spring herbs, 62-3
sage cream, shallot tarts with, 59-60
salads:
   artichokes, quail's eggs and pecorino, 40
   chicken and tamarind salad, 98
   fillet of beef with summer salad, 149-50
   French bean salad with tarator sauce, 183
   smoked fish terrine and samphire salad, 69-70
   smoked quail and asparagus salad with polenta chips, 99-100
   spice-crusted pork fillet, lentil salad and avocado, 144-5
   supreme of chicken with aubergine fritters and bean salad, 103-4
   Thai seafood salad in chicory, 6
   warm salad of black pudding and apples, 54
   watermelon, chicory and feta salad, 41
salmon:
   potato blinis, gravadlax and citrus basil dressing, 91-2
   salmon steak with sautéed cucumbers and mint, 79
   Singaporean lakhsa, 83
   sugar-cured salmon, sweet potato and Sauternes sauce, 77-8
   see also smoked salmon
salsas:
   salsa verde, 71-2
   sweetcorn fritters and salsa, 193-4
samphire salad, smoked fish terrine and, 69-70
sashimi, finnan, 16
sauces:
   béchamel, 228
   bread, 229
   crème anglaise, 231
   fresh tomato, 228
   red wine jus, 232
   sauce vierge, 230
   sweet chilli dipping sauce, 14
sausages:
   cassoulet, 117-19
   fish sausages with sauce vierge, 86-7
   pheasant breast with sausage and pecan stuffing, thyme jus, 125-6
scallops:
   seared scallops with poori and baba ganouj, 9-10
   stir-fry of duck and, 134
sea bass roll with beetroot gnocchi, 93-4

seafood:
   bouillabaise with rouille, 73-4
   Thai seafood salad in chicory, 6
shallot tarts with sage cream, 59-60
sherry, pork chops with chestnuts and, 162
shiitake mushrooms:
   rabbit and shiitake terrine, 50-1
   saddle of lamb stuffed with spinach and, 138-9
shrimps, potted, 28
Sicilian hare with chocolate, 168
Singaporean lakhsa, 83
sloes:
   sloe gin, 233
   venison daube with sloes, 165
smoked cod's roe with pak choi and black beans, 95
smoked eel on latkes with rocket and beetroot relish, 84-5
smoked haddock:
   celeriac crisps with finnan sashimi, 16
   glazed smoked haddock with mustard cream, 68
   smoked fish terrine and samphire salad, 69-70
smoked quail and asparagus salad with polenta chips, 99-100
smoked salmon blinis, 20-1
smoked trout:
   smoked fish terrine and samphire salad, 69-70
soufflèed crêpes with apple caramel sauce, 207-8
soups:
   lobster bisque, 58
   parsnip and porcini soup with mustard and chive sabayon, 52-3
   roast squash soup and Parmesan wafers, 46-7
   sprout and chestnut soup with truffle oil, 57
   vichyssoise with oyster and caviar, 24
spice-crusted pork fillet, lentil salad and avocado, 144-5
spinach:
   grandmother's handkerchiefs, 172-3
   plantain and spinach curry, 191
   saddle of lamb stuffed with shiitakes and, 138-9
   spinach and ricotta malfatti, 34-5
   supreme of chicken with aubergine fritters and bean salad, 103-4
   tarragon chicken with mushroom 'boxes', 132-3
spring onions, white radish cake with bean sprouts and, 179-80
sprout and chestnut soup with truffle oil, 57
squash:
   pattypan squash braised with rosemary and white wine, 182
   roast squash soup and Parmesan wafers, 46-7
   steamed squash with coconut and ginger custard, 203
squid stuffed with its tentacles and prawns, red wine sauce, 81-2
starters, 23-60
stews:

INDEX   247

bouillabaise with rouille, 73-4
   mackerel and chick pea stew, 96
strawberries, pavlova with passion fruit and, 212
stress-free Christmas turkey, 135-6
strudel, apricot, 221
sugar, spun, 217-18
sugar-cured salmon, sweet potato and Sauternes sauce, 77-8
summer pudding with real vanilla ice-cream, 205-6
sweet potatoes:
   sugar-cured salmon, sweet potato and Sauternes sauce, 77-8
sweetcorn fritters and salsa, 193-4
Swiss chard fritters, 188

T
tagliatelle:
   kidneys with green peppercorns and fresh noodles, 169-70
tahini:
   baba ganouj, 9-10
   pitta crisps with houmous and tahini yogurt, 19
tamarind:
   chicken and tamarind salad, 98
   tamarind water, 231
   Thai yellow bean cakes with tamarind dip, 175
tapenade, chargrilled tuna loin with salsa verde and, 71-2
tarator sauce, French bean salad with, 183
tarragon:
   John Dory with chicory and tarragon sabayon, 80
   tarragon chicken with mushroom 'boxes', 132-3
tarts:
   dark and white chocolate tart, 226
   deep raspberry tart, 209-10
   lime tart with passion fruit sauce, 198-9
   'punkin' pie with Bourbon cream and candied physalis, 213-14
   rhubarb and almond cream tart, 200-1
   shallot tarts with sage cream, 59-60
   tarte Tatin niçoise, 26-7
   tartlets of avocado mousse and quail's eggs, 15
   tomato and basil tart, 185
tempura, prawn, 13
terrines:
   guinea fowl, leek and potato, 29-30
   rabbit and shiitake, 50-1
   roasted pepper and aubergine, 36-7
   smoked fish, 69-70
Thai menu, 240
Thai roast duck curry, 124
Thai seafood salad in chicory, 6
Thai yellow bean cakes with tamarind dip, 175
thyme:
   cannelloni of hare and, 166-7
   thyme jus, 125-6
timbales, pepper-lined, 86-7

tiramisù with white chocolate, 222
tomatoes:
   bouillabaise with rouille, 73-4
   cassoulet, 117-19
   fresh tomato sauce, 228
   mackerel and chick pea stew, 96
   panzanella, 33
   sauce vierge, 230
   tarte Tatin niçoise, 26-7
   tomato and basil tart, 185
tongue:
   pressed ox tongue, my grandmother's way, 153-4
tortellini of crab with chervil butter sauce, 65-6
trout:
   trout fillet with oregano crust and smoked chilli sauce, 75-6
   see also smoked trout
truffle oil, sprout and chestnut soup with, 57
tuna:
   chargrilled tuna loin with salsa verde and tapenade, 71-2
turbot with peas, broad beans and asparagus, 64
turkey, stress-free, 135-6
24 carat brûlée, 202

V
vanilla ice-cream, 205-6
vegetables, 171-96
   root vegetable gratin, 196
   stuffed vegetables, 174
   vegetable couscous, 186-7
   see also artichokes; tomatoes *etc*
vegetarian menu, 238
velvet chicken with pineapple rice, 128-9
venison daube with sloes, 165
vichyssoise with oyster and caviar, 24
vinaigrette, basic, 229
vindaloo, authentic pork, 146-7

W
wafers, Parmesan, 46-7
walnuts:
   French bean salad with tarator sauce, 183
wasabi, prawn tempura with, 13
watercress:
   rabbit on watercress with a port sauce, 140-1
watermelon, chicory and feta salad, 41
whisky:
   Bourbon cream, 213-14
white radish cake with bean sprouts and spring onions, 179-80 wicked chocolate brownies, 204
wild boar sauce for noodles, 160-1
wine:
   beef fillet with red wine jus and wild mushrooms, 163-4
   lamb shanks in red wine with champ, 155-6

long-cooked leg of lamb in red wine, 158-9
pattypan squash braised with rosemary and white wine, 182
red wine jus, 232
salmon steak with sautéed cucumbers and mint, 79
squid stuffed with its tentacles and prawns, red wine sauce, 81-2
sugar-cured salmon, sweet potato and Sauternes sauce, 77-8

venison daube with sloes, 165
wine buffs' menu, 237
wontons, duck and ginger, 14

Y
yellow bean cakes, Thai, 175
yellow curry of aubergines, 195
yogurt:
    pitta crisps with houmous and tahini yogurt, 19